Sleep and Dreams

Sleep and Dreams

RUDOLF STEINER
SELECTED TALKS
1910–1924

Edited and Introduced
by Michael Lipson

STEINERBOOKS

Copyright 2003 by SteinerBooks

Published by SteinerBooks
P.O. Box 799
Great Barrington, MA 01230

www.steinerbooks.org

Library of Congress Cataloging-in-Publication Data

Steiner, Rudolf, 1861-1925.
  [Lectures. English. Selections]
  Sleep and dreams : a bridge to the spirit : selected talks, 1910-1924
/ Rudolf Steiner ; translated, edited, and introduced by Michael Lipson.— 1st ed.
    p. cm.
  Includes bibliographical references.
  ISBN 0-88010-512-7
  1. Dreams. 2. Dreams—Religious aspects. 3. Dream interpretation.
I. Title.
BF1091 .S715213 2003
299'.935—dc22
                        2003014936

10 9 8 7 6 5 4 3 2 1

Printed in the United States of America

Contents

Introduction

MICHAEL LIPSON

WHAT ARE DREAMS? Every age, every culture, perhaps even
every person, has a different answer. They agree at least on this:
that dreams are *other*. Their presence in our lives demonstrates that
we are not limited to a single mode of consciousness. The world of
sleep is largely a blank for us, an abyss of non-consciousness yawn-
ing between one day and the next. But the very fact that we can
dream announces our potential for some kind of awareness within
the abyss.

Most cultures have gone further, and noticed a cluster of questions about the nature of reality posed by the un-consciousness of
sleep and the other-consciousness of dreams. Are there worlds more
lively and real-feeling than this one, just as this one sometimes feels
realer and more lively than dreams? Can we be sure that dreams are
less valid in some way than our waking lives? Am I dreaming even
now? To what realities might I someday awaken? Can I extend my
nighttime consciousness beyond dreams to illumine and include
the rest of sleep? Our capacity to sleep and dream thus poses some
of the same questions as our capacity to die.

Rudolf Steiner wrote and spoke voluminously about sleep and dreams. He described them not statically, but developmentally. That is, he saw sleep and dreams as ever-changing phenomena that undergo an evolution both within humanity as a whole and in the course of the natural or meditative development of the individual. To understand the unique quality of Steiner's writings and lectures about dreams, it will be helpful first to bring to mind some of the vast cultural sleep- and dream-lore that acts as the filter through which his views come to us.

The currently reigning theory of dreams in the scientific community of the Northern, Western world presents them as a kind of epiphenomenon. On this view, dreams reveal nothing significant about the individual, and they open no window onto other worlds. They have nothing to do with creativity. The work of J. Allan Hobson expounding this position has been widely disputed but also widely accepted, if not in detail then as a whole. His notion is that, on waking up in the morning, we make a relatively coherent story out of the quasi-random chemical/electrical discharges of the brain during sleep. There is therefore no dream as such, no narrative that arrives within you as a whole. Rather, on waking up you piece together into a semblance of narrative, with one part of the brain, what another part of the brain has disgorged during the night.

Such a reductionist view—reducing the lived experience of the dream to events in the brain—fits well with the tendencies of our age. For we tend to ascribe everything to a physical cause, whether it is disease, fate, intuition or aggression. We like to explain away mysteries as something ultimately measurable, visible, even palpable. Sorrow as well as joy gets overlooked as lived experience and instead is attributed to brain events, which we can induce or dampen through drugs. We feel we are somehow on more solid ground when we can point to childhood vaccination, or environmental pollutants, or brain chemistry, or economic factors, or libido, to explain whatever we do not understand. All unawares, we cut back the realm of the meaningful until we have shrunk the significance of the universe to somewhat less than our own size.

Still, there is that nagging *experience* of dream life that resists reduction to brain events. When we dream, we have the persistent sensation of having left ordinary consciousness behind, of having entered another kind of being. This other world, with its changing moods and tones and images, suspends the rules of workaday life. On the one hand, the images of everyday life may be present, but they combine and vary in ways we never see while awake, with sudden shifts the waking world never allows. On the other hand, our self-experience during dreams is also unusual. We have access there to feelings of great intensity, but often with a diminished sense of personal coherence. Many people, for example, notice they have no feeling of their own body in a dream, or they feel that the body is changed.

Until recently, the dominant Western explanation for dreams in all their variety and peculiarity derived from Freud's psychoanalytic stance toward dream interpretation. For Freud and his professional progeny, the dream presents fragmentary symbols of the dreamer's own repressed wishes. The dream, like a hysterical symptom, allows partially back into consciousness what our inner censor had wished to keep out—mostly our socially unacceptable wishes in the direction of sex and aggression. In his desire to prove every dream the expression of a wish, Freud went to great explanatory lengths. While sex and aggression, as the ultimate ground of dreams as of all other experience, seemed to anchor them in the world of physical, scientifically confirmable "reality," Freud was enough of a psychologist never to be able to demote dreams to the level of external reality. In some places, he almost seems to claim for the unconscious (as the source of dreams) an alternate reality just as valid as sense reality. Here, he puts the idea most strongly:

The unconscious is the true psychical reality; in its inner-
most nature it is as much unknown to us as the reality of the
external world, and it is as incompletely presented by the
data of consciousness as is the external world by the communications of our sense organs. (*Interpretation of Dreams*,
1899)

In most cultures and at most times, the dreams worth talking
about have originally been understood to derive not from the past
thoughts or wishes of the Freudian dreamer, and certainly not from
the agitated brain of the Hobsonian dreamer, but from a world of
super-personal truth whose pathway into a person's awareness is
lubricated by the unusual state of consciousness we enter in sleep.
We *go* somewhere in sleep, and the dream is an expression of that
journey. Such an understanding informs, for example, the Hindu
approach to dream interpretation, the Jewish, Biblical approach to
dreams and the ancient Greek concept of the therapeutic or healing
dream. It is also to be found in shamanic dream journeys in archaic
cultures around the world. In all these traditions, dreams contain
messages from a higher order of being. They are meaningful, and the
meaning is in line with the divine order. One can therefore ask for
a dream, as we might ask for the opinion of another person or being,
and receive it as a generous communication. "An uninterpreted
dream," the Talmud says, "is like an unopened letter." We know that
the ancients were aware of dreams that were mere dreams, phan-
tasms and regurgitations of the day, but they didn't bother much
with them. They only took the trouble to record what Jung called
"big" dreams: those whose vast, expressive source was beyond doubt.

In her wonderful study of Hindu dreams, Wendy Doniger
O'Flaherty offers an example from the dream-within-the-dream
genre. She recounts an ancient tale in which a monk imagines what
it would be like to live as an ordinary layman. "As soon as he had

this idea, his thought somehow took the form of another man. . . . This dream man, Jivata, enjoyed himself for a long time in a town made in a dream. There he drank too much and fell into a heavy sleep, and in his dream he saw a Brahmin who read all day long. One day, that Brahmin fell asleep, and . . ." Men in this story dream their way into being other men or women, animals or even plants who dream or meditate or die back into one another in a dizzying spiral. Finally, someone dreams of Rudra (God), who then enters the cycle and eventually pierces all the levels of illusion. Each dream, each reality, is both honored as sufficient unto itself and also subsumed within another reality from which perspective it is illusion. The process is so self-reflexive, so bewilderingly multi-directional, that the act of awakening from a dream and the act of falling into a dream merge into a single act. By the time you have read the whole narrative (it would have been told or sung aloud in ancient times), you find you have lost your footing in your everyday reality. And that is the point. Such a dream's pedagogical effect is to question all dualistic realities, all "worlds," and yet to affirm the *persons*, both divine and human, who grow through dream levels like lotus flowers emerging from watery depths into light and air.

Dreams in the Bible have a different style from Hindu dreams of this kind. They tend to promote a single level and a single message, but it is always a meaning from on high. The dream message is therefore a reality, never "merely" a dream. Its meta-message is not that all is illusion, but that all is real. The first such dream was the most fateful. An ancient tradition has it that as Adam slept (Gen: 2:21), he dreamt of Eve, then awoke to find her actually there, drawn from his side. Most instructive for us is the account of Pharaoh's dream, interpreted by Joseph (Gen. 41). Pharaoh had his gaggle of wise men, after all, but their interpretations were wrong in the case of this particular dream, and Pharaoh *felt* their wrongness. As when we cannot remember a name, but we know the first names we come up with are wrong, Pharaoh could not interpret his own dream, but knew the suggested interpretations missed the mark. When Joseph offered his interpretation about the seven fat years followed by the seven lean years, Pharaoh instantly recognized it as correct. This is an interesting example, too, because it suggests a universality and democracy imbuing the world from which the divine truths come. Here was a Hebrew slave, after all, in touch with the source of truth that had been attempting, through the dream, to inform an Egyptian king. The capacity to interpret dreams correctly, to see the truth through them and not be misled by their accidental forms, is understood by Pharaoh as a closeness to God. He has no hesitation in putting Joseph at the head of all his kingdom, and renaming him "Zaph-nath-pa-a-ne-ah": *God speaks and he lives.*

It has long been known that sleep is healing. The spiritual alienation of our contemporary hospitals is proved in part by the way that they constantly frustrate sleep, and so delay the healing they supposedly exist to promote. As James Joyce suggests in *Portrait of the Artist as a Young Man*, Hell itself is a place where there is no sleep. In Steiner's work we will see a partial explanation for just why sleep should be so healing. For the moment, we can note the tradition of the healing dream specifically induced in the Greek temple of Asclepius at Epidaurus. There the sufferer would perform ablutions and prayers and fasting, under the guidance of temple attendants, specifically to bring about a dream that the priest would interpret to devise a treatment regimen. On the one hand, this procedure reminds us that it was not always for the laymen (as it was not always for the Pharaoh) to interpret their own dreams. A dream's significance was more apparent to those whose entire lives were devoted to immersion in the divine sources of significance. On the other hand, this system of healing is also an example of the dream *induced.* As in some archaic cultures like the Senoi, the Asclepian dream came not only through a reaching down, from the heavens toward us, but also through an intentional reaching up, from the Earth to the heavens.

Garfield and Stewart have reported on the Senoi dreamers of the Malayan peninsula. There, children report dreams every morning at breakfast. The fathers and older brothers in the family interpret every dream and give advice about how to handle similar dreams in the future. For there, the negative or nightmarish quality of dreams is understood to be an expression of the dreamer's personal attitudes and experiences, which can be intentionally transformed into a gift from another world. Thus, if a child reports a frightening dream of falling, the father may counter that that is a wonderful dream, and ask where the child fell. The child replies, perhaps, that she fell nowhere, but just experienced a frightening sensation. The father then corrects her:

> You must relax and enjoy yourself when you fall in a dream. Falling is the quickest way to get in contact with the powers of the spirit world, the powers laid open to you through your dreams. Soon, when you have a falling dream, you will remember what I am saying, and as you do, you will feel that you are travelling to the source of the power which has caused you to fall. The falling spirits love you. They are attracting you to their land. . . .

As Stewart comments, "the astonishing thing is that over a period of time, with this type of social interaction . . . and advice, the dream which starts out with a fear of falling changes into the joy of flying."

The whole premise of dream interpretation in the Senoi culture is that our dream life lies under our own control. Spiritual progress depends upon directing the course of the dream, at least to a certain extent. Something similar can be found in other archaic cultures, such as the Kogi of Colombia, who make no sharp distinction between what we might call dreams and what we might call visions, but whose dreamers also submit their dreams to the tribe's elders for a kind of spiritual coaching.

A reflection of archaic cultures' approach to intentional dreaming has emerged in our own day in the form of what is known as lucid dreaming. The term refers to those dreams in which the dreamer awakens and recognizes the dream to be a dream *without leaving the dream landscape.* That is, one can become aware that the scene before one is a dream, yet remain in the dream. You know you are asleep in bed, but you have no sensation of the body lying there. To an outside observer you would still seem asleep. The brain registers "REM" or rapid-eye-movement patterns. Your own experience, however, is of intense wakefulness. Such a state challenges our notions of the distinction between sleep and waking; you are awake, but asleep. Advocates of lucid dreaming include Patricia Garfield and Stephen LaBerge, who have written extensively on the theme. With consciousness comes control: At the point of awakening within the dream you also find you can direct the dream events to some degree. Interestingly, as with ancient and archaic dreamers who induce or manipulate dreams, modern lucid dreamers have also noted that there is a limit to what they can do once awake within the dream. For example, you may decide to go for a drive in your car but instead a magic carpet appears at your feet. The possibility of control leads to all kinds of abuses, of course. One lucid dreaming book was promoted through an exhoration appearing on the cover, "Make love with the partner of your choice!" Perhaps the most spiritually minded of all lucid dreaming authors to date is G. Scott Sparrow, whose *Lucid Dreaming: The Dawning of the Clear Light* specifically uses the state of heightened wakefulness in dreams to come unstuck from the world of ten thousand things, and to unite knowingly with the sources of knowing.

My own experience while inducing lucid dreams led to a discovery that approaches the area of dream understanding Steiner tried to convey, for he often emphasized the fluid source of dreams as more significant than the ordinary remembered sequence of dream images. I was awake in my bed, fresh from a dream, and trying to recall the dream in reverse order. I had schooled myself to ask: "What happened before that? And what happened before *that?*" This is a standard technique to recapture more of one's dream after awakening, which in turn is part of the practice of lucid dream induction. On this particular occasion my effort of memory "missed," so to speak, and instead of landing on the previous dream image or event, I discovered a streaming current of meaning whose end result was the dream image. I found myself laughing aloud at the poverty of the normal dream, which is such a small, rigidified extract from this streaming current. In an instant, the project of "dream interpretation" was put into a completely different perspective, since it typically takes as "the dream" only this tiny extract.

Imagine someone in a canoe on a vast river. The person reaches down into the water with a cold spoon. The spoon is so very cold that the spoonful of water immediately freezes within it into a little oval nugget. This frozen nugget corresponds to the normal dream image. The flowing river in its vastness is the real dream, the dreaming behind the dream, never found in normal dream consciousness. Just as silly as it would be for the canoer to say, of the frozen nugget, "Here is the river!"—that is how wrong it seems, after beholding the inflowing dream stream itself, to say of any image or even any sequence of images, words and feelings, "Here is the dream."

Steiner's approach to dreams included elements of all the approaches discussed so far. We should realize, though, that for Steiner the changes in one's dream life that come with initiation, for instance, are a kind of side effect. Though he advocated taking control of one's dream life to some extent, he never promoted dreaming as a spiritual path in itself. By and large, he regarded dreams as too unreliable, too unstable, at least in the long initial phases of personal development, to be more than indicators of a progress whose central focus should be our most light-ful, wakeful function of conscious thinking.

In the written works, Steiner definitely makes the analogy of sleep to death, and sees dreaming as a kind of initial sally of consciousness into the night. He often emphasized a parallel between dreaming and feeling (in both, we are semi-awake) and between dreamless sleep and willing (in both, we are totally unconscious). The direction of human development is toward awareness, awakeness, so that in the long run we are to become, through our own efforts, *continually awake*. In principal, this alertness can extend not only throughout the night, but throughout our "death"—the period between dropping this physical body and perhaps taking up a new one.

To understand Steiner on sleep and dreams, we need to be clear on the topic of "bodies." Steiner described the human being on Earth as comprised of several bodies or systems of organization. These include the physical body, the etheric or life body, the astral or soul body and the I. Sleep, disease, death, meditation and other phenomena involve interactions among these members, all of which are invisible except the physical body. In a kind of symbolic shorthand, Steiner often seems to be discussing the bodies and their interrelationships in spatial, temporal, quasi-physical terms. Yet his work abounds, too, with warnings precisely *not* to take this shorthand for an adequate image of the processes under discussion. Even the physical body, as understood in meditative perception (*cf.* Kühlewind, *From Normal to Healthy*), is not out there apart from us, as a spatially extended thing that exists without our cognition of it. Ultimately, all these bodies, the physical included, are divine meanings, complex words. They are not things but utterances of the spirit, which we can sully or ennoble through the way we understand and intend them. To picture them as things in space, like clouds of light, for example, is to import materialist ways of thinking into the spiritual realm. Still, since it is very hard, perhaps impossible, to describe or discuss them adequately in terms of consciousness alone, Steiner indulged his readers and his audiences in physicalist imagery.

For the most part, Steiner's early writings describe the processes of sleep and dream with broad brushstrokes, while his lectures over the years fill in the details of the picture.

In his early classic *How to Know Higher Worlds* (1904), Steiner entitles one chapter "Changes in the Dream Life of the Esoteric Student." Such changes are a symptom rather than something to be sought in themselves:

> Whereas our dreams formerly only contained echoes of our
> daily lives, and transformed impressions of our surroundings
> or our own bodily condition, the images we now see arise
> out of a world unknown to us before.

Steiner points out something special about the symbolic nature of dreams. He first gives examples of the "sense impression dream" whereby the dreamer experiences, in the dream, a transformed version of what is occurring at that moment in the bedroom or within the range of the dreamer's bodily senses, like a noise outside. Though trivial in itself—the striking of a clock, for instance, may evoke in the dreamer images of soldiers marching to the beat of a drum—this is important because it shows the dream as an altered version of something that is really happening. Though at first our dreams only symbolize in this way the physical events that surround us, or that occur within our bodies, and perhaps also the residue of the day behind us, the symbolizing function of dreams leads further. In the course of esoteric development our dreams will come to symbolize spiritual events that are at least as real as the striking clock but that normally escape both our daytime and our sleeping awareness.

> At this point, then, we begin to have experiences inaccessible to ordinary waking consciousness. But we should never for a moment believe that true mystics, if they experience something of this order in a dream, take such dream experiences as the basis for an authoritative account of the higher worlds. Such dream experiences should only be viewed only as the first signs of a higher development.

The reason we cannot rely on dreams is that the window or organ of the dream has not yet become clear enough faithfully to perceive what lies beyond the dreamer's own "bodies." Steiner goes on to give a hint in the direction of lucid or Senoi-like dreaming:

> We begin to remain awake, in the full sense of the word, during our dream life; that is, we begin to feel ourselves lords and masters of our pictorial representations.

We become increasingly masters *of our representations*, not of that which they represent. The dream, as a window on the objective spirit, begins very unclean, so that we see in it only our own image and the smudged markings of normal sensory experience, but it is a window that gradually grows clearer, so that it can more validly transmit something beyond the dreamer.

Interestingly, the bulk of the short chapter on "Changes in the Dream Life of the Esoteric Student" is devoted not to dreams or sleep at all, but to awareness of the true Self. It is as if Steiner cannot linger on the relatively dubious area of dream without fortifying the subject who dreams. As in all his work, the drive to investigate the true Self or "I" masters others considerations.

A fuller and fundamental description of the state of sleep appears in the 1909 *Outline of Esoteric Science* in the chapter, "Sleep and Death." There, Steiner describes the partial dissolution of the human being that actually constitutes sleep. The principle of life that maintains our vegetative existence (what Steiner calls the life body or etheric body) continues to permeate and regulate the physical body as it lies in the bed. But the essence of the person, the awareness itself, the "I," is no longer present to the body, no longer looking out of those eyes or hearing out of those ears. This "I," along with the organization of inward feelings known as the soul body or the astral body (sometimes translated as the "starry" body), is directed elsewhere. Therefore, using his imagistic shorthand, Steiner describes sleep as the state in which the I and the astral body separate out from the etheric and physical bodies, which are left behind in bed. Such a schema corresponds, at least, to our everyday sense that a person asleep in bed is an earthly and living being (physical and etheric) but strangely devoid of the deciding, feeling person (I and astral) that makes him or her *that* person during normal waking consciousness and activity.

It is lucky for us, in Steiner's view, that the etheric body remains connected to the physical during sleep. "If the physical body were left to itself, it would have to disintegrate." And this separation of physical from etheric is what we call death. There, the I and the astral body depart (as in sleep) but the etheric or *living idea of life* also leaves the physical, and the formerly inhabited body succumbs to merely chemical and physical laws. We normally perceive nothing during death, according to Steiner, just as we normally perceive nothing during dreamless sleep. For consciousness to arise in these states, further esoteric training is required.

Normal dreaming actually represents a refinement on this idea of sleep as the total separation of astral from etheric and physical. For a dream to come about, a portion of the astral must still be connected to the etheric, so that the etheric can make conscious some of what the I and the astral body are experiencing:

> In order for . . . dreamless sleep to set in, the astral body must have withdrawn from the ether body and the physical body. During dreams it is separated from the physical body in that it is no longer connected to our sense organs, but it still maintains a certain connection to the ether body. That we can perceive the astral body's processes in image form is due to this connection. When it ceases, the images immediately sink down into the darkness of the unconscious, and we have dreamless sleep.

Hard as it may be to follow a passage of this kind, it would be much harder if Steiner had dispensed with his imagistic shorthand of "bodies" and described every aspect of the process as the relative interpenetration of living, self-evident ideas. This would be more like a continuation of his epistemological style in works like *Intuitive Thinking as a Spiritual Path* and *Truth and Knowledge*, but it would have become impossibly unwieldy for the kind of detailed spiritual description Steiner was attempting to undertake.

We should note that Steiner's description of dreams corresponds to the current state of neurophysiological dream exploration in that he sees dreams as a borderline, borderland phenomenon. It has been shown that dreams largely take place during the state of REM ("Rapid Eye Movement") that occurs only in relatively light sleep— on the way down to, or up from, the dreamless states marked by slower (*e.g.*, delta) brain waves. This is just what we might expect from a partial involvement of astral with etheric and physical on the way down to, or up from, the dreamless states marked by more complete separation of these "bodies."

In the lectures that follow, Steiner takes the hints and broad strokes of these early writings and expands upon them for the sake of a particular lecture series or "cycle." We have excerpted the most suggestive and important of such lectures for this collection, but they by no means exhaust the richness and variety of his comments on the theme. In each case, a more complete understanding of the given lecture can be gained by reading the lecture cycle from which it came. All our reading of Steiner, as of other demanding texts, will be valuable to the extent we can read meditatively rather than informatively.

Georg Kühlewind has written suggestively on the nature of meditative reading in his *From Normal to Healthy*. Rather than summarize that advice here, I offer an image. Once, on vacation in Maine, I sat down on the porch of our cabin and opened at random a book on the wild birds of North America. The book fell open to the page on the ruby-throated hummingbird. Just at that moment, a ruby-throated hummingbird flew up (from where?) to sip at the geranium next to my chair. When a book is approached in the right way, and when grace meets the reading, it is not *about* anything. Rather, whatever is being described appears, in living reality, before the reader.

It may be helpful, as you read Steiner's accounts of what takes place within and between the "bodies" and other facets of the spiritual worlds, occasionally to engage in the kind of translation that puts apparently physicalist descriptions of spiritual phenomena back into the language of consciousness. This would mean, in first order, to recognize that movement in the spirit is always a matter of attention. When the astral "leaves," "departs" or "moves away" at night, nothing physical goes anywhere. The only thing that can move in space, the physical body, just lies there in bed. Instead, the vector of feeling-attentiveness (astral body) orients toward a different zone of experience from what is made available to it through the senses dur-

xxii *Sleep and Dreams*

ing the day. This turning of attention *is* the astral body's movement. One aspect of the total reality of the world is ignored, another comes into view.

As you read the very detailed descriptions that follow, you might also keep in mind that, in the long run, the investigation of sleep is meant to take us beyond *this* kind of movement altogether, this turning of attention from one thing to the next. We are to graduate from partial awareness, from turning this way and that in sleep/wake, live/die cycles. Through his intimate examination of sleep, of death, of human organization, of our relatedness to other beings and of the great world events, Steiner's life's work was meant to provoke us toward the state of solar activity James described:

> Every good gift and every perfect gift is from above, and cometh down from the Father of lights, with whom is no variableness, neither shadow of turning. (James 1:17)

BOOKS CITED

Cartledge, Paul, ed. *The Cambridge Illustrated History of Ancient Greece*. Cambridge: Cambridge University Press, 1998.

Ereira, Alan. *The Heart of the World*. London: Cape, 1990.

Freud, Sigmund. *The Interpretation of Dreams*. New York: Avon Books, 1965.

Garfield, Patricia. *Creative Dreaming*. New York: Ballantine Books, 1974.

Hobson, Allan J. *Dreaming: an Introduction to the Science of Sleep*. Oxford: Oxford University Press, 2002.

Kühlewind, Georg. *From Normal to Healthy: Paths to the Liberation of Consciousness*. Great Barrington, MA: Lindisfarne Books, 2000.

LaBerge, Stephen. *Lucid Dreaming: The Power of Being Awake and Aware in Your Dreams*. New York: Ballantine Books, 1985.

Mallasz, Gitta. *Weltenmorgen*. Einsiedeln, Switzerland: Daimon Verlag 1996.

O'Flaherty, Wendy Doniger. *Dreams, Illusion and Other Realities*. Chicago: Chicago University Press, 1984.

Sparrow, G. Scott. *Lucid Dreaming: The Dawning of the Clear Light*. Virginia Beach: A.R.E. Press, 1976.

Steiner, Rudolf. *How to Know Higher Worlds: A Modern Path of Initiation*. Christopher Bamford, trans. Great Barrington, MA: Anthroposophic Press, 1994.

Steiner, Rudolf. *Intuitive Thinking as a Spiritual Path: The Philosophy of Freedom.* Michael Lipson, trans. Great Barrington, MA: Anthroposophic Press, 1994.

Steiner, Rudolf. *An Outline of Esoteric Science.* Catherine Creeger, trans. Great Barrington, MA: Anthroposophic Press, 1997.

Steiner, Rudolf. *Truth and Knowledge.* New York: Garber Communications, 2000.

Stewart, Kilton. "Dream Theory in Malaya" in Charles Tart, ed. *Altered States of Consciousness.* New York: Anchor Books, 1972.

Van Eeden, Frederik. "A Study of Dreams," *Proc. Soc. Psych. Res.*, Vol. 26, 1913, pp. 431-461.

Wangyal, Tenzin. *The Tibetan Yogas of Dream and Sleep.* Ithaca, NY: Snow Lion Publications, 1998.

Watson, Gay, Stephen Batchelor and Guy Claxton, eds. *The Psychology of Awakening.* York Beach, ME: Samuel Weiser, 2000.

CHAPTER ONE

The Secrets of Sleep

FOR STEINER, THERE is never any complete human unconsciousness. We may not be self-aware at all times, but we continue to exist, as
spiritual, meaning-oriented beings, actively engaged with our surround-
ings, through the day, through the night and even through death. There
is no condition in which we are not present.

We are unaware of this continual presence, however, just as we are
unable to see our own face unless we look in a mirror. During our night
journeys, we are unaware of ourselves until we wake up in the morning
and our body, with its brain, provides a kind of "mirror" to the soul.

With an exact capacity to describe phenomena as they arise, Steiner
refers to experiences anyone can have during the process of falling
asleep—processes, he emphasizes, that are not so exalted or distant from
everyday awareness. On falling asleep, the physical body and its senses
grow dim, but a moral awakening occurs, and the soul reviews the day,
seeming to spread out in a vast moral universe. We can think of it, perhaps, as a world of love.

We learn here about the increasing sensitivity of the spiritual
researcher, who begins to sense the greater mobility, fluidity of thinking
available in the dream state and, by contrast, the positive resistance to

this flow that the brain offers. As Steiner points out, we normally have no awareness of our body or our brains; with training, we begin to perceive its real nature and even to work on its structure by the very path of development that helped us to perceive it.

Reality, in its fullness, is infinitely more than what we perceive through the normal sense organs. To open our senses on the world is almost to close them to the spirit, though the proper education of the senses allows them to let in the creation as sacred light. Experiences during sleep, when attention is withdrawn from the senses, can be an introduction to the world of true reality (c.f. the use of this phrase in Intuitive Thinking as a Spiritual Path).

The analogy of the horse and rider appears in the text and clarifies the situation. The soul/spiritual aspect of the human being gets off the body, like a rider getting off a horse, so that it can be refreshed for the next day's battle. Steiner develops the theme of the rejuvenation of the body that can take place through sleep precisely because we leave the physical and etheric bodies alone.

We need the physical body to mirror, and so make conscious, our experience of the sensory world. In the same way, we use the other, finer "bodies" to mirror successive spiritual worlds. The higher "mirrors" that help us to become conscious of higher worlds are not physical in any way. They are made of our own intense attentiveness, our spiritual activity.

BERLIN, NOVEMBER 24, 1910 GA 60

GA numbers refer to volumes in the complete German edition of Steiner's works, published by Rudolf Steiner Verlag in Dornach, Switzerland.

It is natural for the official science of our time to say very little about the phenomena of sleep we will be addressing today. Yet everyone should feel that sleep is something that comes into our lives and presents us with the greatest riddles of our existence. People have always felt that there was something both mysterious and significant about sleep, and have called it at times the "brother of death." Today, we will limit ourselves to a consideration of sleep itself. Other lectures will return us again and again to the nature of death.

All that we count as our soul's experience in an immediate sense, all of the ideas that well up and fade away from morning to night, all our sensations and feelings that make up the drama of the human soul, all pain and suffering, even our impulses of will—these all sink into an indistinct darkness when we fall asleep. And many philosophers don't know what to do with the fact that, when they talk about the nature of the soul, the nature of the spirit, they have to admit that every day, no matter how well thought out their ideas and concepts about it, no matter how well they investigated it—it all seems to dissolve into nothing when we sleep. If we think of our souls the way both scientists and non-scientists do today, we have to say that they are extinguished, they go away, during sleep. For someone who only thinks of the soul in terms of the body, the full riddle of humanity only appears on deeper reflection. For the truly bodily functions, bodily activities, continue during sleep. Only what we call the soul's functions seem to cease during sleep. It merely remains to ask if "body" and "soul" have been properly understood by thinking that what is extinguished during sleep is really the full extent of the soul. And perhaps, quite apart from spiritual science or anthroposophy, ordinary observation can show us that the soul is active even during sleep. To gain some clarity about these concepts, to evalute the phenomena of life properly in this area, we have to provide ourselves with some precise concepts.

As an introduction, let me say that on this theme, as on others, spiritual science or anthroposophy is not in a position to speak in the general sort of way that is so beloved today. If we speak today about the nature of sleep, we will be speaking about human sleep. For spiritual science knows very well, as we have pointed out in regard to other areas, that what may appear as similar phenomena in various kinds of creatures can derive from very different causes in the different cases. We have suggested as much for death, for the whole spiritual life, and for the nature of spiritual life in animals and humans. It would lead us too far afield to speak today about the sleep life of animals. So we want to state in advance that everything said today will apply to human sleep.

As human beings, we are able to speak about the phenomena of our own souls because, as we all know, we are aware of what we think, what we will and what we feel. Now the question must arise— and it is an important one for our investigation today: Are we justified in using our concept of normal contemporary human consciousness to account for all the phenomena of the human soul and the spirit? To express myself more clearly on this point, let me make use of an analogy. You can wander around a room and never see your own face until you pass in front of a mirror. Isn't there a big difference for you between walking around the room on your own and seeing what you're doing in the mirror? Something like this goes on in human consciousness, in a different sense. We can live the life of our souls, and only know about it, only become aware of it, if a kind of mirror is held up to us. For instance, we can very well imagine that the life of the human soul continues on regardless of whether we are awake or asleep, but that the state of waking consists in our perceiving our own soul life through a kind of mirroring—let us say, a mirroring within our bodies. We don't perceive the life of our soul while in a state of sleep because it is not mirrored in our bodies.

With this idea, not much is proven, but we gain two concepts. We can now distinguish between the life of the soul as such and the self-aware life of the soul. And we realize that our awareness, our knowledge of the life of the soul normally depends on its being mirrored by our body, since we can know nothing of it if it is not mirrored. The unmirrored state would be something like sleep. Now, having gained these concepts, let us call to mind the phenomena of our waking and sleeping life.

Anyone who can really observe life can clearly sense, or *see*, how the moment of falling asleep actually proceeds. We can perceive how the images and feelings grow dimmer, losing their intensity. But that is not the essential thing. While awake, we live in such a way that our whole mental life is kept in order by the self-aware I; we combine all our ideas through our I. If we could not, while awake, unite our ideas through our I, we would not be able to lead a normal mental life. We would have a group of images, ideas, that we would relate to ourselves, that we would call our own, and another group that we would see as something alien, like an outer world. Only people with a split personality experience this diseased condition with the mental life torn apart into various components. For normal people the essential thing is that all their images and ideas are related to the perspective of a single point: the self-conscious I.

At the moment of falling asleep, we can clearly feel how the I is at first overwhelmed by images and ideas, even though these are growing dimmer. The images and ideas assume an independent life, forming into something like separate clouds at the horizon of consciousness, and the I is lost within them. Then we feel how the sensations of seeing, hearing and so forth become duller and duller, and finally how our impulses of will grow weak. And now we must begin to allude to things that have been clearly observed only by very few.

We feel that, while we saw things with definite outlines during the day, at the moment of falling asleep it is as if we were enclosed within a kind of fog that seems cold or offers other feelings at certain points on the body: on our hands, our joints, our temples, our spine and so on. These are feelings you can actually observe while falling asleep. They are, so to speak, the trivial experiences that you can have every night as you go to sleep, if you want to.

There are better experiences to be had by people who observe the moment of falling asleep more exactly as a result of a more delicate development of their soul life. Despite falling asleep, they can observe a kind of waking up at the same time. And what I am telling you now can be confirmed by anyone who has acquired the proper methods, since they are universal human phenomena. At the moment of sensing that there is a kind of waking at the very moment of falling asleep, we can say that it is as if our conscience expands, as if the morality of the soul wakes up. This is a fact. And we can then observe just what it is, from all we have experienced the preceding day, that we are morally satisfied with. We feel it most strongly at the moment of this moral awakening.

At the same time, this kind of feeling is the opposite of daytime feeling. During the day, our feelings show how things come toward us. On falling asleep, we feel how our soul pours itself out within a world of ever-expanding conscience and inwardness. Then there is a moment—which can seem much longer to the person falling asleep—of inner blessedness if the soul feels itself in accord with what it finds as it spreads itself outward. And there is often a deep feeling of being torn asunder if the soul has something with which to reproach itself. In short, the moral self, suppressed during the day by sense impressions, expands and feels its own self more strongly at the moment of falling asleep. And anyone with a method or even a sense for this kind of observation knows that at this moment a yearning arises that could be described as follows: You want to have this moment stretch out indefinitely, and never to end. Then a kind of jolt comes, an inner movement. It is very hard for most people to describe, though spiritual science can do so exactly. It is a kind of demand that the soul makes of itself: "You have to spread out further! You must pour yourself out still more!" But in giving itself this requirement, the soul is lost in the moral life in its environment. It is as if you put a tiny colored droplet into water and let it dissolve. At first you still see the color, but when the droplet has spread throughout the water it becomes fainter and fainter and finally is no longer present as a color at all. This is how it is for the soul: as it begins to spring up and live in its moral mirror it still feels itself; after the jolt, the inner movement comes, this feeling ceases like the droplet that loses itself in the water.

This is no theory. It is observable and accessible to all, just as every natural scientific observation is accessible to anyone. If we observe the process of falling asleep in this way, we can say that the human being grasps something at the moment of falling asleep that cannot remain in awareness afterward. In terms of our earlier comments, we could say that we have a moment of leaving the mirror of the body that mirrors the phenomena of life. And since we have not yet developed any other kind of mirror, we stop perceiving what we are.

Now, if we are not too stubborn and narrow-minded about the darker mysteries of the soul, we can understand the events of the day in a particular way. For example, I have often mentioned that if someone has to memorize something, to learn it by heart, it is much better to "sleep on it." Fending off sleep is the real enemy of memorization. The possibility of learning by heart is helped by sleep, which makes it easier than if you try to learn something at one go. This applies to other activities of the soul as well. And we can convince ourselves very easily that, if we didn't have the state of sleep in our lives, it would be impossible to learn anything at all, to take in anything for which the soul's contribution is necessary. The natural conclusion to be drawn from such phenomena is that our soul has to withdraw from the body from time to time to draw strength from a region outside the body, because the forces in question are actually used up as long as we stay in the body. We have to imagine that when we wake up out of sleep in the morning, we have brought strength with us from the state we were in; strength to develop capacities that we couldn't develop if we were only tied to our body. So the effect of sleep is evident in our normal lives, as long as we think straightforwardly and aren't too obstinate.

Those who stand firmly in ordinary life may need to muster considerable good will to observe as a coherent whole what appears self-evident to someone who has gone through a developmental process to perceive spiritual life. I would like to put forward something now about what happens when a person develops those powers that slumber within the soul, so as to perceive without the use of the senses, and comprehend without normal reasoning. For the time being, I would like to emphasize just a few of the experiences a person can have after going through such exercises — exercises that actually provide the soul with spiritual eyes and spiritual ears. They enable us to look into the spiritual world, which is not the object of any speculation but is just as much an object as the colors and forms, warmth and cold and sounds are for those who perceive by the usual senses. Earlier lectures have already shown how to arrive at true clairvoyance. This spiritual development, these exercises, consist in our drawing something forth from within ourselves and gaining new organs of cognition. We have to leap beyond the soul in its normal state and perceive a world that is always around us but that in our normal state we cannot perceive. If you do undertake such exercises, your sleep life will change, as all who arrive at real spiritual research are aware. I want now to speak of the first state of alteration within the sleep life of the truly clairvoyant spiritual researcher.

When we first begin to do spiritual research, we don't feel so very different from how we are in normal consciousness. For at first the exercises allow us to sleep just as unconsciously as anyone else. But the moment of waking up in the morning does reveal to the practitioner something quite special. I want now to portray these phenomena, which are altogether concrete. Suppose we do the exercises and then think very exactly about something. And we try, since we may have a very hard problem before us, to strain all our spiritual energies to arrive at a solution. The same thing can happen that happens to many a school child: our spiritual forces aren't sufficient to complete our task. Now, if through our exercises we have developed more ability to experience the connection between our inner state and our bodies, then we feel something special when we are unable to do something. We feel a new kind of resistance in our physical organs, for example in our brain. We actually feel how the brain is opposing us, as if we were using too heavy a hammer to strike a nail. The brain starts to be a reality for us. Normally, when we use our brain we have no sense of it as an instrument like a hammer. As spiritual researchers, however, we feel our brains; in fact, we feel ourselves independent of our own thinking. It is a direct experience. But when we cannot solve our problems, then we feel that certain activities we have to carry out while thinking can no longer be carried out. We feel very clearly that we are losing control of our instrument. This is a fact that we can experience very exactly.

Now, when as spiritual researchers we sleep on a problem and then wake up, it can often happen that we suddenly feel equal to our task. But at the same time we feel that just before waking we did something, we worked on something. We feel that while asleep we could bring something within us into motion, into activity. While awake we were forced to use our brain. We know that. We could do nothing else while awake. Yet we couldn't use it properly; the brain gave resistance, as I have described. But we feel that in a state of

sleep we were not so involved in the use of the brain. We could cre-
ate a certain motion without the brain—which would be too tired,
or overtaxed. Now, on waking, we feel something unique: we perceive the activity we practiced in sleep, though indirectly. The Lord
does not give unto his own during sleep, after all. We are not spared
the effort of finding the solution once we have woken up. The solution might just occur to us, but normally this isn't how it works,
and particularly not for things that do after all have to be solved by
the brain.

We then feel something previously unfamiliar in the world
of the senses, namely, we feel our own activity, as if it were alive
in front of us in pictures, strange pictures that are in motion, as
if the thoughts we need are like living beings that have all kinds
of relationships with one another. So we feel our own activity
during sleep—you can call it the activity of thinking—as a
sequence of images. This feeling is hard to describe because you
are *in* it in a special way. You tell yourself, "That is you, yourself!" On the other hand, you can also distinguish between this
feeling and yourself very exactly, just as you can distinguish
between yourself and an outer movement you make. So you have
images, imaginations, from an activity you carried out before
awakening.

And now you can notice, if you have learned to pay close
attention to yourself, how these images of an activity from
before awakening begin to unite themselves with our brain and
make it into a more moveable, adaptable instrument. As a result,
you are able to carry something to its conclusion as you could
not before because of the resistance—for example, to think certain thoughts. These are delicate matters, but without them you
cannot arrive at the secret of sleep. You do not feel as if you have
performed an activity like those you do while awake, but rather
an activity that reconstitutes certain things in the brain that

were worn down and couldn't be built back up previously. You feel like a craftsman working on your own instruments.

This makes for a considerable difference in how you feel about any activity of the day. Normal daytime activities give us a feeling like that of sketching something according to a model. In that case I am forced to guide myself with every stroke or dab of color by the model I have before me. But for the things that appear as images at the moment of waking, and that represent in a sense an activity during sleep, you have the feeling that you were inventing the brushstrokes yourself, and creating the figure from out of yourself, without being bound to a model. This phenomenon reveals what the soul did before it woke up; it shows the activity of regenerating the brain. You gradually come to realize that what feels like covering the brain with newly drawn figures is really a rebuilding of what was destroyed in the brain during the day. You begin to seem to yourself like your own architect.

Now, the real difference between any normal person and a spiritual researcher who can perceive such things is only that the spiritual researcher does perceive them, while the normal person cannot. For the same activity carried out by the spiritual researcher is carried out by everyone, only our awareness normally doesn't catch the moment of building organs anew during sleep.

Let us take such an experience and compare it with what we spoke of earlier, the dulling and darkening and diminishment of the images of daytime as we fall asleep. This latter phenomenon can really only be seen in the proper light if you either liberate yourself from the views that are supposedly based on today's natural science, or else really go into the results of the nature research of our time. The more exact thinkers can only conclude from current brain research, for example, that the evidence points to the independence of our souls from our bodies. And it is very interesting that a popular book recently came out in which the sources of our mental life, of our spiritual life, are portrayed backwards, with no understanding. The book, *Man and Brain*, by William Hanna Thomson, contains much that is very clever. It goes into current brain research and very instructive issues like the phenomena of tiredness, which I have often pointed to.

As I have shown, muscles and nerves only grow tired through conscious activity. As soon as our muscles serve exclusively organic activity, they cannot grow tired. It would be too bad, after all, if your heart muscle and other internal muscles had to take a rest. We only grow tired if we carry out an activity that is not inborn in the organism, an activity that belongs to the conscious life of the soul. This is why we have to say that if the life of the soul were born in us in the same way as the activity of our hearts, then we couldn't account for the enormous difference in what does and does not grow tired. And so the author of the book is forced to admit that the soul relates to the body as a rider does to a horse; the soul is quite independent of the body. For someone based in natural scientific thinking, this is quite an admission! So the image is something like a centaur, as these were conceived in ages when people could see into the spirit. Today, many feel differently. One man suggested to me that the Greeks saw another, mounted tribe like the Skythians from afar and in the fog; they couldn't clearly distinguish the shapes they saw and thought the men's torsos grew out of the horses. Explanations like that may suit a materialist. But it is precisely the natural scientific research of the present that compels us to acknowledge the independence of the soul from the body.

We can investigate this area best if we call to mind phenomena that may be rare, but nonetheless cannot be denied. We are all aware, for example, of that case of the simple country fellow who, on his deathbed, began to speak in Latin—which he had never spoken, but which he had heard only once, long ago, as a boy in church. This is no fairy tale, but a reality. Of course, he had not understood it when he heard or recited it. From this we have to conclude that the environment has an effect on us that is quite different from the effect it seems to have on ordinary consciousness. What we receive into our normal consciousness depends on our upbringing, our education and so on. But we unite inwardly not only with what we understand; we take in infinitely more than what we are aware of. We can even observe how, for certain people at certain times, ideas emerge that they had formerly paid no attention to and had no memory of. Yet certain events can evoke them so they even come to the forefront of consciousness. We have to admit that the whole of our inner life encompasses much, much more than what we take into our daytime awareness. This is extraordinarily important, since it makes us turn our attention to something within us that has scant effect on our bodily nature, because it remained unconscious, but lives on in us nonetheless.

Our view is directed to the subterranean aspect of our soul's life, which actually has to be present in every reasonable human being. For every reasonable human knows that our conscious awareness of the world depends on our sense organs and on what we can understand. No one is justified in limiting reality to what we can perceive. It would be illogical to deny the existence of a spiritual world, since we can only speak of what we do see and hear and think, but we can never judge what we cannot perceive. For the world of reality is not the world of what we can perceive.

The world of what we can perceive is limited by our sense organs. That is why we can never speak, in the Kantian sense, of limits to cognition, or to what we can know or not know. We can only speak in accordance with what our perceptual organs reveal to us.

When we consider this, we have to say that behind the tapestry of the sensory world, behind what the sense of warmth perceives as warmth or cold and so forth, there lies a limitless reality. Can we really suppose that only the reality we perceive has an influence on us? The only logical view is that our perception gives us a portion, a piece of the whole reality, and that behind what is given to us through our perception there lies a limitless reality—which is real for us, too, since we are within it—that lives on for us, living and surging and having an influence on us.

So what is our waking life? We have no choice but to say that we open our senses, our cognitive capacity, to an immeasurable reality that we confront. Through having eyes that work in just this way, ears that work in just that way, a sense of warmth and so forth, we present ourselves with a particular portion of reality. The rest we reject, as if warding it off, and exclude it from ourselves. In what, then, does our conscious activity consist? It consists in our warding something off, our closing ourselves off from something. And when we strain our sense organs, we are holding off something not perceived. What we perceive is merely a vestige of all that surrounds us and that we largely kick away. We feel ourselves actively present in the world, united with the world. Yet through our sensory activity we ward off the majority of impressions because we cannot endure the whole immeasurable infinity, and only allow in a piece of it. If we think in this way, we have to imagine quite different relationships between our whole bodily nature and the outer world than those we can perceive or understand with our reason. Then we are not so far from thinking that these relationships we have in the outer world live on in us; that the invisible, supersensible or extrasensory is active in us; that the extrasensory, active within us, uses our senses to construct a sample of the whole immeasurable reality.

But then our relationship to reality becomes something completely different from what we can perceive with our senses. It is then as if we had to come before a mirror and say to ourselves, "At base, you are something completely different." The mirror only shows you the form, and perhaps the colors, but inside you are feeling, inside you are thinking, and the mirror cannot show any of that; it can only show what its laws allow it to show. How you are as a soul with regard to your organism is something very different from what your senses show you. They limit you to what *their* laws allow. So by facing the world, as when looking into a mirror, you meet a world that is only possible due to the configuration of your senses.

If you think this thought through to the end, you will no longer be surprised that finally our waking consciousness depends very much on the organization of our sense organs and our brain, just as what we have before us in a mirror depends on the characteristics of the mirror. Someone who looks in a funhouse mirror and sees the caricatured face it reflects will happily admit that the image depends not on himself or herself, but on the mirror. So too all that we perceive depends on the workings of our mirror apparatus. And our mental activity is limited, as if reflected back within itself, by mirroring itself on our bodily life. So we ought not to be surprised that the portion of reality that we see depends, as can even be shown physiologically, on our body. For everything the soul does depends on the organization of our body if it is to come into consciousness. Observation shows us that concepts we simply constructed to begin with really do correspond to the facts. The difference is that our body is a living mirror. The mirrors we normally look into remain unchanged by our looking into them. To be sure, there is one thing about the mirroring that we can change: if we breathe onto a mirror it no longer reflects properly. But the mirroring that goes on in our body, which experiences the activity of our soul, is itself an activity, a process within our body. What we pose before ourselves as a mirror is itself an activity.

It is as if we were writing down what we think, and then the letters appear before us in our body. We write the activity of our soul into the life of our body. If you confirm this anatomically, you will only find the letters, the outer apparatus, for our soul's life is not completely observable if we only look at the body; we only see it entirely if we see it independently of the body. This is what the spiritual researcher can do, observing the life of the soul as it begins to mirror itself at the moment of waking into day consciousness. The life of the soul is like an architect who builds something during the night and deconstructs it during the day.

So we have before us the life of the soul in waking and in sleep, and we see that in sleep the soul is independent of the life of the body, as a rider is independent of a horse. But as the rider uses the horse and uses up its strength, so the soul uses up the activity of the body, so that chemical processes take place as the letters of the soul's life. In this way we come to a point where we have used up the body's life, limited as it is by the senses and the brain, to the point where we have exhausted it. Then we have to begin the other activity, introduce the opposite process, and build up again what we have destroyed. This is the life of sleep. So from out of the soul we exercise two opposite activities on our body. While awake we have around us our world of shifting thoughts, of pleasure and pain, our feelings and so forth. But we are thus using up our body's life, actually destroying it continually. While asleep, we are the architects, building up again what we have destroyed during our waking life.

Now, what do spiritual researchers perceive? They perceive the architectonic activity, the building-up activity, in characteristic images of movements that swirl within themselves: a real process that is the opposite of normal waking life. It is no fantasy when in these inwardly self-active movements we recognize the mysterious process the soul carries out in sleep, and that consists in our reconstituting what we destroyed during the day. This is why sleep is both curative and necessary.

But why are we unaware of our own sleep? For that matter, why does waking life come into our awareness? It is because the processes we carry out in the daytime are something like mirror images. But when we practice the other activity, the reconstitution of what has been worn out, we have nothing for it to mirror itself on. We lack the mirror for it. Again, it is only spiritual science that can show what is at the root of this. After a certain point in our research, we not only experience the activity of the soul as I have already described it, as a dream memory out of sleep, but we experience it as if we are being directed away from the instrument of the body to perceive an activity that plays itself out in the spirit alone. At that point you can say to yourself, "Now you are not thinking with your brain, but you are thinking in quite other forms; now you are thinking in images that are independent of the brain." But we can only arrive at this point if we experience that the whole nebulousness that surrounds us as we fall asleep does not disappear; rather, this fog, perceptible at our temples, our joints, our spine, becomes something that reflects itself—just as we can see our whole body reflected—if it can limit its own activity and take it back into itself.

The whole difference between real clairvoyance and normal, waking daily life consists in this, that waking consciousness needs a different mirror for the soul's activity to come into consciousness, and uses the body for this purpose, while the activity of the clairvoyant, shining forth as soul activity, is so strong that its rays are drawn back into themselves. We are mirrored in our own experience, in our spiritual organism. Fundamentally, our soul lives within this spiritual organism at night even if we are not spiritual researchers. The soul pours itself out into this spirit. We won't really understand what sleep is until we realize that our bodily processes—all that anatomy and physiology can investigate—do nothing but provide a mirror for the processes of our soul, and that these soul processes live in a spiritual existence between falling asleep and waking up again. If we think about it any other way we go astray. So we have to refer to this secret life of the soul that never enters into the awareness mediated by the body. And when we see long-ignored ideas crop up in someone, we have to say that something must be present in the human being that is different from the ideas of conscious life.

Now, as I have hinted in the past, it is child's play to refute the realities of spiritual research. Nonetheless, they are true. Spiritual science speaks of our having a human physical body that can be seen with the eyes and touched with our hands, the body familiar to anatomy and physiology. In addition, as another member of our human nature, we have the astral or astral body, the bearer of all we take into awareness, of everything that we experience during daily life as mirrored on the body. Between the astral body and the physical body there lies something else, which is the bearer of those ideas that remain unconscious for years, and which then are taken up by the astral body and can come fully alive. In short, we say that between the astral body, the bearer of consciousness, and the physical body, the ether body or life body is active. This life body is not only the bearer of such unnoticed ideas, but it is what builds up the whole physical body.

Now, what is happening during sleep? The astral body, the bearer of consciousness, along with the I, leaves the physical and life bodies so that there arises a split within our human nature. As long as we are awake, the astral body and I stay in the physical and life bodies, and the processes of the physical body act like mirroring processes through which everything that happens in the astral body comes to awareness. Consciousness is the mirroring of experience through the physical body, and we must not confuse conscoiusness with the experiences themselves. When the astral body leaves during sleep, it is not able, in normal people, to perceive anything in the world of the stars. We are unconscious.

What ability must the spiritual researcher acquire to be conscious of things during sleep without relying on the brain? We have to acquire the ability to perceive in something, to reflect our soul's activity in something, that lives and weaves between things in such a way that it is perceptible during waking consciousness in the same way as our own life body. The life body is woven from the very medium through which a clairvoyant perceives; so that for the clairvoyant the outer world becomes a mirror, just as for the soul life of the normal person the physical body is a mirror.

There are intermediate states between waking and sleeping. One such intermediate state is the dream. Spiritual research reveals that dreams arise in something like the same way as clairvoyance, only clairvoyance is schooled, while dreams come from fantasy. By leaving with the astral body, we lose the capacity of mirroring our soul life through the physical body. But through certain abnormal conditions that arise for everyone, we can acquire the capacity to mirror our experiences through our life body. We have to see the life body, like the physical body, as a mirror, though as long as the sensory world affects us it is only the physical body that operates as a mirror. But when we become silent within ourselves, and think through the impressions the outer world has made on us, then we are working within ourselves, and our thoughts are real. We live our thoughts, and feel that we are relying on something finer than our physical body, namely our life body. It is then the life body that mirrors itself in us, during those solitary musings that do not depend on any outer impressions. In waking consciousness, however, we stay in our life body; we perceive what mirrors itself there, but not the activity of the astral body. When we are in the intermediate state between waking and sleeping, without being able to receive sense impressions but still able to receive something connected to our life body, then the life body can mirror for us what we are experiencing in our soul with our astral body. This is what dreams are—which, because we are in an otherwise unfamiliar situation, demonstrate such unruliness.

When we consider all this, much that is mysterious about dream life becomes clear. We have to think of the foundations of the life of the soul as closely connected to the life of dreams. While the physical body mirrors the life of our soul and our daytime interests, our life body connects us to distant experiences that may be far behind us and that can only come to awareness faintly because daily life makes such a strong impression on us. If we really observe our dreams well, then we can notice many strange things about them. For example, a good composer has the image of a devilish figure playing a sonata for him. He wakes up and can even write the sonata down. Something was active in him that seemed external, alien. There was something ripe within the composer's soul that could not make its way into waking consciousness because bodily life is only a hindrance and not apt to mirror it. In fact, this hindrance is the whole point of bodily life. After all, we need "hindrances." When a train travels over the tracks, it is the hindrance, the friction, that enables it to move; without friction, the wheels can't turn. Our bodily processes meet our soul life as hindrances, and these hindering processes at the same time are mirroring processes. If we are ripe for something in our soul and haven't greased the wheels of our machine enough, then waking consciousness sabotages our awareness. But when we leave our phyiscal body, then our life body—which has to appear as something alien, since it is of a much more delicate nature—can express what lives in the soul. If it is strong enough, it forces its way into our dream life, as it did in this case of the composer. It has less to do with our daytime interests than with hidden interests that lie further down, in the delicate substrate.

It is the same in the following case. (By the way, I am only recounting something that has really been observed.) A woman dreams—though she has a husband and children whom she loves very much—that she is engaged a second time and goes through all the consequent experiences with great pleasure. What is she dreaming? She is dreaming of experiences that lie far away from her current life, which she went through long ago and no longer recognizes, because our normal daily affairs are only connected with our physical body. What still lives on in her in her life body is mirrored there as a result of some other event, perhaps some happy sensation that provoked the dream.

A man dreams that he is going through experiences of his childhood. And these childhood experiences go on in the most amazing way. A particularly important and deeply felt event wakes him up. At first, the dream is dear to him; he goes to sleep again and dreams on. A whole suite of unpleasant experiences now marches through his soul, and a particularly painful one wakes him up. All of it is very far from his current daytime experiences. He gets up, shaken by the dream, walks about in his room for a while, then lies down again and now experiences in a dream events that he has not experienced before. All the events he has gone through get confused and he experiences something new. The whole of it becomes a poem, which he later writes down and sets to music. This is a true story.

Now the concepts we have gained will help us to see what has happened. For the spiritual researcher the matter appears as follows. The man experienced an interruption in his development at a certain point of his life. He had to give up something important to his soul. But when he did so, it didn't disappear from his life body. It was simply repressed by normal life. And, since it had a certain inner elasticity and strength, it forced its way out in a dream, at a time when we are free of the hindrance of waking life. So the man in question was really close to what expressed itself in the poem, to that which had been drowned out by waking life.

So the dream shows us very clearly the independence of the life of the soul from the outer life of the body. And this is compelling evidence for the idea of the mirroring of the soul's life through the body. The very fact that the interests we are so involved in do not imprint themselves directly on our dreams shows that alongside everyday life there runs another life, which, as I have said, to a more conscious, more delicate observation appears as a kind of awakening. In that region there lives everything of our spirit that is independent of the life of the body—for example, our conscience. But in the daytime, this other life is limited by our daily interests. In sleep, our soul is completely filled by this moral quality. We really live our way into the spirit, which we can characterize as an inner shift, a movement. What we call spiritual scientific research is something through which we *consciously* live our way into the world that normal people live into unconsciously every time they fall asleep.

People will gradually have to become aware that the world is much broader than what we can understand with our senses and our reason, and that the life of sleep is something we need because in waking life we wear down precisely our noblest organs, which serve our conceptual life. In sleep we reconstitute them, so that they can face the world in strength and power, and reflect our soul life back to us in waking daytime life. Everything characteristic of the life of the soul could become clear to us in this way. Who doesn't know that after a good, deep sleep we feel tired out? People often complain of this, but it is not a sickness; it is very understandable. For the healing power of sleep is only really felt an hour or an hour and a half after waking up. Why? Because we have worked well on our organs, so that they will work not just for a few hours but for the whole day. And immediately upon waking we are not *in* them enough to use them, but have to slip into them and really use them only after some time. In the case of a certain kind of tiredness, we have to be glad that in an hour and a half we can feel our way back into our restored organs. For sleep gives us what we need, the architectonic powers for the organs we have depleted during the day.

So we can say that our soul life is a life of independence, a life of which we have a mirror image in our daytime consciousness.

Consciousness is a mirroring of the soul's relationship with its environ-
ment. In waking life we are lost in our environment, in something
alien to us; we are immersed in something we ourselves are not. But
during sleep, and this is the essence of sleep, we withdraw from all
outer activity to work on ourselves. The right analogy is a ship that
is used for the voyage on the high seas and gets repaired and refur-
bished when it comes to harbor. Anyone who thinks we do nothing
during sleep could also believe that nothing is done to a ship at harbor. But it does have to set sail again, and then you will see what
happens if it doesn't get repaired first. That's how it would be with
us if our soul were not worked on during sleep. We are given back to
ourselves in sleep, while during the day we are lost in the external
world. A normal person, however, is not able to see what the soul
does during sleep in the same way that we can observe the outer
world during the day.

We shall see in the lecture "How to know higher worlds" that
there is a kind of mirroring cognition in the spirit as well. Through
this, we can perceive in higher worlds. This shows us that when the
soul is unaware of itself, it knows nothing of its own activity. Yet it
is involved with itself, works on itself, and independent of the body
receives the power that it needs to build the body back up again.

We can summarize what we have said and characterize the
essence of the soul in words that take what we know of sleep as a
foundation for much of spiritual science:

Wrapped around by sleep, the soul returns itself to itself—fleeing
to the spirit's distances when the narrowness of the senses
becomes oppressive.

CHAPTER TWO

Sleep and the Three-Part Soul

~~~~~~

FOR THIS LECTURE, *it is worthwhile to know in advance that Steiner will be discussing the relationship of sleep in its phases to the qualities of consciousness he called "souls."*

In everyday language, we are used only to speaking about "soul" in general, or about a person's individual "soul." Steiner referred to soul as the "spirit's own life" within the individual—the way in which the universal truths become conscious to the individual. He particularly works out this definition of soul in Theosophy. In that book, as in Outline of Esoteric Science, he distinguishes among the different developmental stages of consciousness. One kind of "soul" follows another, both in the development of the individual person and in the development of humanity.

Thus, we first have a "sensitivity soul" that transmits sensations, then a "rational soul" that mediates reason and feelings, then a "consciousness soul" that has self-awareness. The whole of humanity, for Steiner, is now in the age of the consciousness soul, which necessarily includes the other three; an individual matures to the point of the consciousness soul at about the age of forty-two. All these are given to humanity and to the individual. From this point on, however, it is up to us to develop further.

Steiner goes further and declares a link between stages of sleep, or death, and the meanings borne by the planets. In this way, he paints a picture of an interconnected world, in which as living, sleeping and dying human beings we are not wandering alone and apart, but participating in what Dante called "the love that moves the Sun and the other stars."

VIENNA, MARCH 22, 1910 GA 119

. . . Through sleep, we draw the power we need to build up our souls in waking life. But such things are much more complicated than we tend to think. Today, based on spiritual research, we have something more exact to say about the difference between waking and sleeping. First, let me just remark that we need not list all the more or less interesting hypotheses put forward by the physiology of the present to explain these states. We could list them easily, but it would only distract us from actual knowledge. We will only point out that the ordinary natural science of our day can merely investigate what has been, so to speak, left behind in the physical world—the physical body and life body.

What spiritual science investigates is completely alien to natural science. But from its own standpoint, natural science has a certain right to be one-sided. For the "I" and the astral body—which are what the spiritual researcher investigates, and what lift themselves out of the physical and life bodies during sleep—are only observable in the spiritual world. Later, when the person wakes up, they enter the physical world, as if they have dipped down into the physical and life bodies.

Now, we want to consider this sleeping human being. It is quite natural for normal consciousness to assume that the sleeping human being is something unitary. We don't investigate further. We don't ask ourselves whether the person who has entered the spiritual world during the night is subject only to a single force that pervades the spiritual world, or whether the person may be subject to the influence of many forces that act upon the body-free soul.

Can we distinguish between the various forces to which we are exposed during sleep? Indeed we can; there are very different influences that do not at first make their impression upon what lies in the bed, but rather upon the human soul itself, which has lifted itself out as the astral body and the "I." We will approach these influences upon the sleeper through familiar experiences and facts.

If we consider a bit more exactly what is happening to us as we fall asleep, we can notice how our external activity gradually diminishes. During the day, we moved our body with the help of our soul; at night, this activity diminishes. A little self-observation at the moment of falling asleep leads to the feeling that our "I" can no longer exercise control over our own limbs. We feel unable to direct the movement of our limbs by means of the will. Then we lose control over what is called speech. Then we feel our capacity to connect to the outer world in any way fall off gradually. All impressions of the day disappear. First the movement of the limbs and the speech organs fades away, then the sensitivity for taste and smell, and finally the capacity to hear. Through this growing incapacity of the soul, we can feel ourselves emerge from our bodily sheath.

With this, we have already characterized the first influence operating on the sleeping human being: namely, the influence that drives us out of our bodies. In self-observation, we can sense this as a power that comes over us. Something comes toward us from another world that drives us out of the physical body. It is not that we command ourselves not to taste, not to hear, and so forth. Rather, there is a power here that makes itself felt. This is the first of the influences from that world into which we dive at night. But if this were all, we would only arrive at an absolutely peaceful, undisturbed sleep. Such sleep does exist, of course. But there are two other possibilities.

First, there is the state of sleep in which more or less chaotic images force their way into our sleep life. There is something else present besides the influence that brings undisturbed sleep, for sleep is interrupted by dreams. So the next-closest influence is that which the world of dreams dangles before the sleeping soul. It imposes the world of dreams into our nights.

Yet this is still not the only way in which our normal sleep can take on a different form. Many of us know another kind of sleep. It is more rare, but it does exist. I mean those times when a person begins to speak or act without any awareness of it. Normally, there is no memory during the day of what impulses may have led to these actions at night. This situation can develop to the point of sleepwalking; the sleepwalker behaves like a robot. While doing so, a person may also have dreams. Still, for the most part there are no dreams, but only robotic action without even a dreamlike awareness of the impulses behind it. Through this third kind of influence, the dreamer enters into connection with the outer world, just as during the daytime, only without awareness. These activities during sleep are subject to a third influence.

We can thus ascertain three influences. Yet these three influences are present not only during sleep but all the time, and spiritual research can confirm that they are present for everyone. For most of us, it is the first of the three that predominates. The second, the dream state, is less often there; it comes and goes. These two are so strong for most people that the third, activity during sleep, is a rarity. Yet even the third is present for everyone. For the sleepwalker, the third influence is so strong, and the other two so weak, that it predominates.

In spiritual science, we have always distinguished among these three influences, and we have to assume three regions within the human soul such that the first region is more subject to the first of these influences, the second region to the second influence and the third region to the third influence. So the human soul is a three-part entity, susceptible to three kinds of influences. We call the first part of the soul, subject to the first influence that drives the soul out of the physical and life body, the "sensitivity soul." The second is known as the "rational soul." The third, because of its peculiar nature, does not reveal itself at all; this is the "consciousness soul." So we must distinguish three influences in the state of sleep; and the three members of the life of the soul, which are subject to these influences, we distinguish as sensitivity soul, rational soul and consciousness soul.

When a person is put into a state of dreamless sleep by a certain power, then something is influencing the sensitivity soul. If dream images permeate the sleeper, an influence is present in the rational soul. If the sleeper sleepwalks, an influence is making itself felt in the consciousness soul. Still, this only portrays one side of the life of the soul during sleep; we have portrayed the person in the process of falling asleep. Now we have to characterize the other side of the life of the soul, the opposite side. Let us consider the human being in the process of waking up, returning to the physical world. What happens when we wake up?

At night, a certain force drove us out. This power can drive us out of our bodies because we are subjected to this power first. In later stages of sleep, we are subjected to the other influences. But once they have done their work, the human being is something different from before; the person has changed during sleep. The change is evident to us in that we were tired in the evening, and in the morning we are once again able to enter into bodily life. When these influences have done their work, we are strengthened, empowered. We have drawn what we need for daily life from the spiritual world. It is above all the influence on the rational soul that strengthens us. But once we are strengthened, the same influence that drove us out of our body then leads us back to it. Its influence is reversed. The same power that drove us out at night—the influence on the sensitivity soul—brings us back in the morning. Everything that has to do with the sensitivity soul was tired in the evening. In the morning, refreshed, we can be interested again in the impressions of the physical world—the colors, lights, objects—so that they fill us with joy and sorrow, with sympathy and so forth. We are involved in joy and sorrow, in the external world. What is ignited in us when we grow interested in the outer world? What is it that feels joy and sorrow? What has interests? That is the sensitivity soul. In the evening, our lively participation was tired, weakened. We feel it refreshed in the morning. In the morning, we feel that the same phenomena of the sensitivity soul, of the life of sensation, that were weakened the previous evening have now come to life again in a fresh way. Thus we come to see that it is the same power that lead us out that now leads us back in.

The waking soul brings us back into life. What at night seemed dead now seems reborn. Only now the person moves in the opposite direction. During the night, a kind of circulation takes place. While going to sleep, we move toward the point where the influence on the consciousness soul is the strongest. After falling asleep and before waking up, the influence on the rational soul is the strongest. Going to sleep and waking up, the influence on the sensitivity soul is strongest.

If we want to draw what happens, we can do it in this way (see diagram)—though it is only schematic. I will designate the moment of going to sleep, when the person is driven out of the physical body

Sleeping

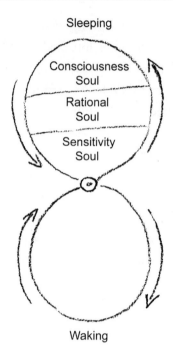

Waking

and into the unconscious, by drawing this point in the center. I show the movement into the state of sleep by drawing a line this way, and the process of waking up as a return out of sleep. I show the course of daytime life through this lower line, and the return toward sleep by this other line. So with this figure eight we have characterized the whole process of waking and sleeping: the upper half shows the state of sleeping, the lower half shows the state of waking.

We have now three forces that affect the human being during sleep. These three have had specific names for spiritual science since ancient times. But one should initially link nothing to these names other than to use them as designations for these three forces. For it is a fact that if you went back into ancient times, you would find that these names were originally given to these three forces, and if they are now used for other things, it is a secondary use of the terms. The force that acts on the sensitivity soul as we go to sleep and as we wake up is called "Mars" in the ancient languages. The force that acts on the rational soul between going to sleep and waking up bears the name "Jupiter." This is the force that drives the world of dreams into the rational soul. The force that, in certain circumstances, wants to make us into sleepwalkers, and affects the consciousness soul, is called "Saturn." In the terms of the ancient spiritual science, then, we can say that "Mars" put people to sleep; "Jupiter" sent them dreams; and finally dark "Saturn," whose influence cannot be resisted, is the cause that agitates them during sleep and makes them act unconsciously.

For the time being, then, we want to take the original meaning of these names, which designate *forces* that act on the human soul during sleep, and not think about their astronomical meanings. When we wake up in the morning, what happens then? We are transferred to a world we normally consider to be our only world. We have sensory impressions. They occur in such a way that we can't see beyond them. They appear to our senses when we wake up in the morning. The whole tapestry of the sensory world lies spread out before us. But we do not only perceive the external world with our senses; we then also have a feeling about everything we perceive. Even if the feeling of pleasure during the perception of a color is very slight, some inner process is still present. All external sense impressions work in such a way as to call forth inner impressions: violet, for example, works differently from red. Such feelings belong to the sensitivity soul. What is conjured up before the soul from the outside is caused by the sensitivity body. It is the sensitivity body that causes us to see yellow or red; but it is the sensivitity soul that causes whatever we inwardly sense and feel about the impression that the yellow or red color makes on us. In the morning, the sensitivity soul begins to be immersed in the impressions of the outer world that it receives through the sensitivity body. What was exposed during sleep to the influence of Mars becomes involved after waking in the external sensory tapestry. Now, we designate the whole external sensory world, to the extent that it evokes certain feelings in our soul, with a special name: the name of "Venus." Yet we should only think of this as what influences our sensitivity soul from out of the external sensory tapestry, which does not leave us cold, but fills us with feelings, with sensations. It is this influence, active from morning on, that we designate as the force of "Venus."

There is another influence from out of the physical world that affects the rational soul. This is the influence by which we can withdraw from external impressions and digest them. There is a difference between the experiences of the sensitivity soul and the rational soul: The sensitivity soul only experiences anything during the time it is devoted to the external world. But when you pay no attention to the external world for a while, and allow external impressions to resonate within you, and think about them—then you are involved in the rational soul. This is more independent than the sensitivity soul. We designate the capacity by which a person can integrate external impressions as "Mercury." During the day, the influences of Mercury play a role. So there is a certain correspondence between the influences of "Mercury" and "Jupiter." For the normal human being of today, the "Jupiter" influence appears within the rational soul in the form of dream images. The "Mercury" influence causes inner thought experiences in the soul.

In the nighttime, in our dreams, we don't know the source of what our soul experiences. During the day, however, we think we know the source of what we think about. But even during the day, there are influences that affect our consciousness soul. What is the difference here? The sensitivity soul is active even if we just stare stupidly at the outer world. When we withdraw from the impressions of the outer world and think them over, then we are involved in the rational soul. But when we take what we have thought over and again turn to the outer world, and again put ourselves in connection with it by our deeds, then we are involved in the world through the consciousness soul. For example: 1. I see the flower. 2. I think about it. 3. I want to make someone happy.

There is a correspondence between the activity of the consciousness soul in waking life and in sleepwalking; however, only in the waking state do we notice that we ourselves are present, as our "I," during our own deeds. At night we are driven along by the dark, obscure power of Saturn. What acts on the human consciousness soul during waking life, in such a way that it can become independent, is called the power of the "Moon."

We have discussed three parts of the human soul. Through these we are subjected to three different influences in the night: the "Mars," "Jupiter" and "Saturn" influences. And when we unfold our soul's life during the day, we are involved in the forces of "Venus," "Mercury" and the "Moon." With this we have indicated the human being's course through all twenty-four hours. We will now bring forward a series of other phenomena that are not usually considered in this connection. Please allow the earlier parts of the presentation to find their full explanation through what comes later.

Let us now consider in a general way the path of the Earth around the Sun. If we do this in the same way that external science does it, we are only at the very beginning of spiritual science. For what takes place in the physical, external world is only a metaphor, an outer image of inner, spiritual processes. What we learn from astronomy about the world of the stars can be compared, in relation to what really underlies the stars, to a child's knowledge of the workings of a clock. We explain to a child what the twelve numbers correspond to, and what the movement of the hands designates. Then the child can tell time. But this has little meaning until the child learns to relate the movement of the hands to what happens in the world. When the little hand points to the six and the big hand points to the twelve, the child also has to know how this hour relates to the sunrise at different times of year. The child has to learn the relationships in the world, and know how the clock is a metaphor for these relationships.

In astronomy, we learn that the Sun sits in the midst of the solar system with the planets surrounding it, and we might learn to read when Saturn or Jupiter is going to be found in a particular corner of the sky. If you know the current position of the planets, you know as much about the firmament as a child does about a clock when the child can say, "It's 9:30." But you can go further and learn about the relationships in life to which the planetary movements correspond. You can learn to understand how the cosmic forces, unseen, operate out of the powers of the macrocosm like a vast cosmic clock. From the "clock" of our solar system you can ascend to the great planetary relationships. Then you can know *why* Venus stands in different relationships to Jupiter at different times. There are reasons why the cosmic clock has been constructed in just this way. The thought of the movement of the planets in our solar system extends and becomes a meaningful thought. The planets become a cosmic clock for us. Otherwise, it would be as if the clock had only been built as a joke, without any meaning.

We can also say that the planetary system, as a cosmic clock, becomes a means of expression for what really lies behind the heavenly bodies of the solar system. First let us consider this cosmic clock in and of itself, as we are accustomed to do in natural science. Then we cannot be met with the reproach that we did not operate scientifically enough. We can easily refute the natural scientific idea that this planetary system was built by itself. According to science, cosmic clouds began to rotate, and the planets formed from out of them. The teacher can show this in an experiment by making a drop of oil rotate. But a clever student might object to this Kant-Laplace theory, and point out that the teacher has forgotten that he or she actually set the oil in motion. The experiment with the drop of oil only shows that something must be there behind what's rotating—forces that cause the movement. In the same way, forces and powers stand behind the formation of the cosmos. The planets, the Earth, rotate around the Sun.

Let us now put the Earth in this position (see diagram) so that the order is Earth, Venus, Mercury, Sun. If the Earth comes around to the other side of the Sun, then the order is Moon, Mercury, Venus. What was called "Mercury" in earlier times is called "Venus" now; what lies close to the Sun is "Venus," what is further away is "Mercury." So we have: Moon, then Mercury, Venus, and beyond the Sun, Mars, Jupiter, Saturn. If we unite these various bodies we have the lemniscate. The Sun becomes the midpoint. There is a possible position of the solar system such that the various planets take on the same spatial ordering as the course of the human being during sleep and waking.

This shows the configuration of planets that exactly corresponds to the varying daytime and nighttime human conditions, taking the

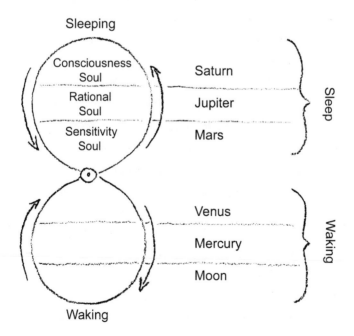

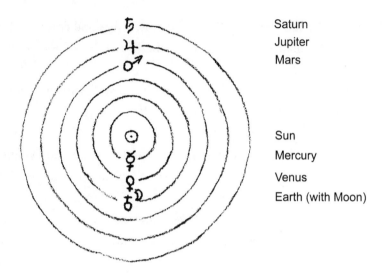

Saturn
Jupiter
Mars

Sun
Mercury
Venus
Earth (with Moon)

moment of falling asleep as the midpoint. We can draw the same schema for the planets and for the daily course of human life.

From this perspective, vast forces underlie the organization of our planetary system. They regulate the vast cosmic clock in just the same way as our life is regulated during every twenty-four hour period. The thought no longer seems absurd that mighty forces operate in the macrocosm, and these are analogous to those which guide us by day and by night. It was from just such thoughts that the same nomenclature arose to designate the forces of the cosmos and those that operate within us. The force that drives Mars around the Sun is similar to that which allows us to fall asleep. The power that pushes Jupiter is similar to that which sends dreams into the rational soul. The force that drives Venus is related to the force that regulates the sensitivity soul during the daytime. Far-off Saturn, with its weak power, behaves like those weak forces that operate occasionally on the consciousness soul of those who sleepwalk. The Moon is impelled by a power similar to the power that orders our daily life with its sense impressions. The distances of space signify something that expresses itself in our own temporal human life as stronger and weaker influences. If we consider, quite superficially, that Saturn is the furthest planet and has the least effect on our solar system, we can then compare it with the dark Saturn powers that have only a slight effect on us. In the same way, the power behind Jupiter can be compared with something else that occasionally comes into our lives: the world of dreams. So we find a remarkable correspondence between the forces that affect human life and the ones that move the great cosmic clock. This is the correspondence of microcosm and macrocosm.

In fact, the world is much more complicated than we think. We can only understand our humanity when we take into account what is within us that relates to the greater world, and compare our inner lives to the course of the planets. This is why the great masters of spiritual research have chosen the same names for the great world and for the small world—the little world enclosed within our bodies.

Today, I could only offer a few distant hints about the correspondence between the microcosm and the macrocosm. I have hinted from afar about the beings who, out of their own forces, regulate the movements of our solar system like the movements of an ordinary clock. We have gazed up toward the borders of the region from which we can hope that the whole spiritual world will open to us. We want to come to know the planets as the cosmic hands of the cosmic clock. And we want to meet the beings who move the planets around the Sun, and who prove to be related to what goes on in ourselves. We want to understand how the human being is born as a microcosm from out of the great world, the macrocosm.

CHAPTER THREE

Sleep and the World of Stars

〰〰〰

SOME VERSIONS OF *spirituality, like some versions of contemporary science, seem to deprive the world of personhood. When, for example, God is reduced to a principle or to a power, we lose the sense of a Person who Speaks: we lose the Word. When every kind of self is denied, when the world of meanings is reduced to a world of things or processes, then our outlook becomes cheapened and theoretical rather than vital and alive.*

Steiner's whole tenor was in the opposite direction: from things to beings. Every aspect of existence that might first seem to be material or abstract becomes personal in anthroposophy. In this lecture, Steiner follows the soul through sleep and waking cycles as it suffers the support and the assaults of various invisible beings who permeate the Earth and the heavens.

Along the way, though only lightly, Steiner will emphasize that the stars and the planets are themselves the expression of supersensible, that is, spiritual, beings. The star followed by the magi was not just a particular physical ball of gaseous matter, but a concentrated, light-like source of meaning, the Person who was to be born. In the same way, the stars and planets as discussed by Steiner are the expression of entities who make living meanings. It is Steiner's outrageous claim to be able to read the outer signs and tell us the particulars of their message.

DORNACH, DECEMBER 3, 1922 GA 219

I would like to make it ever more evident to you that we belong in our essential nature not only to the world of Earth, to earthly existence, but also to cosmic existence, to the existence of the world of the stars. I have already pointed out some of what belongs to this realm. To avoid misunderstanding, I want to preface what I have to say now with a brief remark. If you speak about the connection between the human being and the world of the stars today, you are likely to meet the reproach that you are involved in the dilettantish astrology of our time. But if what I say is properly understood, the great difference may come to light between what is meant here and the dilettantism that nowadays comes up in connection with the ancient astrological traditions.

We say that the human being between birth and death is a being that stands in relationship with the Earth and with earthly events. What do we mean by this? We mean that we human beings have an existence that is owed, first of all, to the possession of a metabolic system, taking in the materials of the Earth as nourishment and processing them in our organism. We mean that through our breathing and all that is connected to it inwardly we are further involved in the Earth, specifically with the atmosphere around the Earth. We may go on to say that we can perceive the Earth through our senses, and we even perceive an afterglow of the extraterrestrial, which by the way is far more earthly than we normally realize. So we can say in general that as human beings we receive earthly existence into ourselves through our senses, through our rhythmic organization and through our metabolism. We have in ourselves a continuation of those processes by which earthly existence itself was animated. But in us, too, there is a continuation of cosmic, extraterrestrial processes. Only we should not think somehow that an influence is exercised upon us by the Moon, by Venus or Mars as planets, as if they sent down rays to permeate us here on Earth. If we say that the human being is subject to the influence of the Moon, we have to understand it as something like what is meant when we say that the human being is subject to the influence of the substances of the Earth.

If you go past an apple tree, pick an apple and eat it, you could say the apple tree has an influence on you; but for that you don't have to imagine rays coming from the apple tree to you. Or if you go past a meadow with an ox in it, and a week later you eat the flesh of this ox, you also wouldn't exactly say that the ox exerted an influence on you. In the same way, you shouldn't imagine too concretely what is meant by saying that the world of the stars has an influence on us. The relationship between the world of the stars and us is really there, just as there is a connection between the human being and the ox that the person has walked past and later eaten.

Today, I have to speak about certain relationships that exist between the human being and the world of the Earth, on the one hand, and extraterrestrial existence on the other. If once again we turn our attention to the human oscillation between waking and sleeping, we notice that, while awake, a person is mostly in a state of exchange with earthly substances and forces. While awake, we perceive through our senses. We don't perceive through our senses while asleep. Normally, it is only while awake that we eat and drink—though some might like to do so while asleep as well. Only the process of breathing, and the closely connected processes of circulation, continue both during waking and during sleep. Of course, they differ in the two states, and I will speak later of how they differ.

For the moment, let us keep to the fact that while awake, we are in a relationship to the outer world through our senses and our metabolism—initially, only in regard to the things we all know about; the point here is to confirm what we already know.

Let us start with the way we take in materials for nourishment from the outer world during the time we are awake. During waking, an inner activity takes place in us as a result of our digestion of what we eat. But we should not forget that, while awake, after having taken in food and while the inner physical and life processes proceed in us as a result, the whole human organism, the physical as well as the life organism, is permeated by the I and the astral body.

In this waking state, the I and the astral body take charge of what happens in the physical and life processes as a result of taking in nourishment. But what happens there as a result of the I and the astral body does not take place during sleep. During sleep, what affects the physical and life bodies is an activity that is not of this world, but proceeds from the cosmic environment of the Earth; it comes from the world of the stars.

We could say—and this is not merely a picture, but a reality— that by day we eat the substance of earthly materials, and by night we take in what the stars have to give us. Awake, we are tied to the Earth. Asleep, we are taken away from the Earth, and heavenly processes play into us, into our physical and life bodies.

Materialistic thinking imagines that when we go to sleep it is only the material we have taken into us that operates within us. In fact, whatever we have taken in, we digest it during sleep through the forces of the Earth's environment, through the forces of the cosmos. Suppose we eat some protein. This protein is only linked to the Earth through our being permeated, while awake, by our soul and spiritual essence, that is, by our I and astral body. During sleep, what affects this protein is the whole planetary world, from the Moon to Saturn, and also the world of the fixed stars. And the chemist who wanted to investigate what goes on in us during sleep would have to know more than earthly chemistry. This chemist would also have to know a spiritual chemistry, since the processes are different than during the day.

It is the same with the I and the astral body of the human, which are separated from the physical body and the life body during sleep. These latter two are not in immediate connection to the world of the stars, but they are indeed in such connection to those entities whose physical images are Sun, Moon, and stars—that is, to the entities of the higher hierarchies. We could say that, while asleep, the human is a duality. Our I and astral body (or spirit and soul) are involved in the spiritual essence of the higher realms of the universe. Our physical and life bodies are involved in the physical image, the physical reflection, the cosmic-physical image of these higher entities. Knowing ourselves as earthly beings, we have actually become, under the influence of intellectualism, more and more like Philistines. We can call our current era the time of intellecual and scientific progress, but we could also call it the time of the progress of philistinism, of materialistic philistinism.

For we are not normally aware of our dependence on anything beyond the sense impressions of the Earth, the rhythmic processes released in us through the processes of the Earth, and the metabolic processes also caused by what is earthly in us. This is why we remain unaware of our place in the universe. And our place in the universe is an extraordinarily complex one. As soon as you take away the veil that is always spread out before us, so that we see both the sensory world and what lies behind it, then life does become an amazingly complicated affair. For one thing, you become aware that it is not only the beings of the stars and their physical reflection that have an influence on human beings. Within Earth's own being supersensible entities are present who are related to the beings of the stars but who have, so to say, pitched their tents in the realm of Earth.

You know that the Old Testament peoples honored Yahweh. This devotion was aimed at a real being. And this being has a connection with what reveals itself in the physical world as the Moon. Of course it is only an imagistic way of talking, but it does have a reality too, if we say that Yahweh resides on the Moon. Everything connected with Yahweh is connected to the Moon.

But there are also beings who, when the Moon parted from the Earth, rejected the journey to the Moon undertaken by the Yahweh beings and stayed in the realm of the earthly. We can, in a sense, feel the Yahweh beings behind whatever we see of the Moon. We can say that they are the outward reflection of what participates in the ordering of the world as Yahweh. But when we learn what lies beneath the Earth's surface, both in solid Earth and in the water, then we find beings who rejected the change of residence to the Moon, and who had the wrongful desire to live on Earth.

Now, there exist helpers for those beings whom I have called Moon beings. These helpers belong both to Mercury and Venus, just as the Moon beings belong to the Moon, so that to some degree the beings of the Moon, Venus and Mercury form a trinity. The well-ordered beings of this kind in our universe belong to these three "stars." But in the solid and watery Earth there are beings of the same category who nevertheless belong in a sense to an earlier era, who did not go along when the Earth became cosmic through the Moon and through Venus and so on.

Now, these later beings also have an influence on the sleeping human being, just as the properly cosmic beings do, only their influence is unhealthy. They have the unwholesome influence I could characterize in the following way. A person falls asleep, and is then in the state between going to sleep and waking up, and just then these unwholesome Moon, Venus and Mercury beings appear and take upon themselves the task of convincing the person that bad is good and good is bad. All this takes place unconsciously between going to sleep and waking up.

This is the shocking, the frightfully painful thing that Initiation brings up: that you come to know things beyond the threshold of normal consciousness that are by no means harmless. In normal consciousness we have no sense of what a person is exposed to between falling asleep and waking up. Yet we are actually exposed to these beings, who try to convince us that good is evil and evil is good. For the earthly, moral ordering of things is tied up with the human life body, and we leave our moral achievements behind in the bed when we fall asleep. We pass over into the state of sleep unprotected by our moral qualities.

Natural science necessarily brushes up everywhere against the things discussed by spiritual science. You may have read an interesting recent report in the newspapers, a statistical finding that is quite correct. The report was that criminals in prison actually have the healthiest sleep; the real hardened criminals are not tortured by nightmares and so forth while they sleep. That only comes up again when they return to their life bodies, where morality resides. It is just the person who tries hard to be moral who may, through the moral constitution of the life body, also take take some of it into the astral body. Such a person is then plagued by dreams as a result of only slight moral lapses. But it is a fact that we take into sleep very little or nothing of the moral constitution we may have attained during our earthly life. And during sleep we are exposed to those beings I have spoken of.

These beings are identical with the ones I have always counted as ahrimanic beings. They have the task of keeping human beings on the Earth as much as possible. You know from the portrayal in my *Occult Science* that the Earth will at some point dissolve and pass over into the state of Jupiter. These entities want to prevent it. They want to prevent us as human beings from developing along with the

Earth in an ordered fashion, so that it can grow into Jupiter. They want to preserve the Earth in its current state of being. That is why these entities continually try their hardest to do as follows. I am speaking here of processes that take place behind the scenes, that have been around as long as there have been humans on the Earth.

As human beings, we shift over in sleep into our starry nature and our nature as I's. Now, every time someone falls asleep, these entities who live illegitimately on the Earth—beings who belong to the Moon, to Venus, and to Mercury—attempt to provide the human being with a life body from out of the life atmosphere of the Earth. They hardly ever succeed, except in rare cases, of which I may speak at a later time. Yet they never give up the attempt, since it always seems possible to these beings, when we have left behind our life body on the bed as we sleep, to surround us and permeate us with another life body made out of the life atmosphere surrounding the Earth.

If such an ahrimanic being did really succeed in gradually providing us with a complete life body in this way, then after death we could maintain ourselves in this body. Otherwise, the life body normally dissolves within a few days. We would be able to survive in our life bodies, and a human race living in such bodies would eventually come about. That is what this particular facet of the spiritual world wants. This would tend to preserve the Earth. It is a fact that inside the solid and watery constitution of the Earth there is a host of beings who would like to gradually transform humanity into ghosts so that the proper goal of earthly evolution cannot be achieved. At night, these beings by no means lose their courage. They always think their attempt will succeed.

We must simply be aware that we human beings have an inadequate power of reason; particularly in our day of advancing philistinism, reason has been developed in a questionable way. We can boast of a certain power of reason, but it in no way reaches up to the point of the reason of these much higher beings who want to achieve what I have just spoken about. We shouldn't tell ourselves that these entities must be very stupid. No, they are not foolish at all. Yet they keep to the belief that they will be able to prevent a majority of the human race from attaining its future state connected to the Earth's incarnation as Jupiter.

If you can see a bit behind the scenes of sensory existence, you can see that these beings do in fact sometimes lose their courage and become disappointed. They do not suffer their disappointments at night, but during the day. You see how these beings experience disappointment when you meet them, for example, in hospitals. For the illnesses human beings suffer have as one aspect that they challenge us to work toward healing with all possible means. But on the other hand we have to ask how states of illness emerge from out of the dark womb of earthly existence. The illnesses that do not come from outer influences, but from within the human being, are connected with the following fact. When ahrimanic beings have nearly managed to provide a given person with a life body outside the normal life body, then on waking such a person carries along the causes of sickness. Through these very causes of illness, the legitimate Venus, Mercury and Moon beings protect themselves from the harmful influence of the illegitimate ones. Indeed, if at times a person did not get this or that illness, the danger I have spoken of would come to pass. The body succumbs to an illness so that the person can (if I may use the expression) sweat out the harmful life processes caused by the illegitimate ahrimanic beings.

Something else that comes up as a kind of reaction in us so that we do not succumb to these ahrimanic influences is the possibility of error. Another is egotism. Of course, we ought not to be sick, ought not to fall into error, ought not to be egotistical in an exaggerated sense. Yet egotism in itself is another way in which we stick to the proper course of earthly evolution, in opposition to the extraction of our human essence by these ahrimanic beings.

This is only one kind of being to be discovered behind the senses of normal sensory life. The other kind we can imagine when we know that we are subject on Earth not only to the cosmic influences of Moon, Venus and Mercury, but also, behind the Sun, Mars, Jupiter and Saturn.

You know from the lectures I gave in the so-called French course that the Moon is the physical reflection of those beings who bring the human being into the physical world. Saturn is the physical reflection of those beings who carry the human being out from the physical world of Earth. The Moon takes us down onto the Earth. Saturn takes us back into the cosmic vastness and from there into the spiritual world. And just as the Yahweh Moon deity has Venus-Mercury beings as helpers, so Saturn has Jupiter and Mars as helpers in this enticement of the human being into the vastness of space and on into the spiritual world. These are again influences that work on us in an opposite direction from the influences associated with the being of the Moon.

It works this way. Up until our seventeenth or eighteenth year, it is above all the effects of Moon, Venus and Mercury that influence us. Later, after we have passed our twentieth or our twenty-first year, we find primarily the influence of Mars, Jupiter and Saturn—which grows, later on, to the point of leading us out of earthly existence and into the spiritual world. Our inner consititution as humans depends on this shift from the inner to the outer planets. For example, up to our seventeenth or eighteenth year we are predominantly dependent on the great circulation of blood that travels throughout the body. Later, we are more involved with the minor blood circulation. These are things that have to be left for later lectures. What interests us at the moment is that, just as the illegitimate beings of the Moon, Venus and Mercury dwell in the solid and liquid components of the Earth, so the illegitimate beings of Mars, Jupiter and Saturn dwell in the air that surrounds the Earth. It is there that they have the conditions they need for being—their "home," so to speak. And these beings too have a great influence on us when we sleep. But the influence operates in the opposite direction.

These beings would like to turn us into moral robots, so to speak, so that while awake we would not listen to our instincts, our drives, the language of our blood. They want us to despise all this, to only obey the Inspirations coming from these illegitimate Mars, Jupiter and Saturn beings, and so to become moral automatons with no understanding of our possible freedom. That is what these beings want, and their influence is uncommonly strong. It is they who try every night to make us accept the influence of the world of the stars, and not return to take in the influence of the Earth. They want to lift us completely away from earthly existence. They want us, and have wanted us from the beginning of human development on Earth, to reject the Earth—the only possible site of our awakening to freedom. Instead, they want us to remain as moral automatons, as we were in the preceding stage of the Earth's metamorphosis, the Moon stage.

We stand right in the midst of these two warring cosmic camps: between those who dwell in the elements of warmth and air, the others in the Earth and in the fluid element. Our physical bodies conceal from us the fact that a fearful battle in the cosmos is being waged over our being. Today, we have to enter into the knowledge of such things, which concern us as human beings, for we are human precisely through our being struggled over by forces in the spiritual world. It is important for us today to understand where we are as human beings.

At some point it will be quite right to disdain our contemporary materialistic way of seeing in comparison with the humanity of the future that knows about the spiritual that lies behind the physical. That will be far more justified than when we say, today, "Ah, how childish were the natural scientific ideas of the ancient Greeks! They were such children; we have come so far since then!" Well, we have come far in our philistinism. Our criticism will be far more justified when we come to a full awareness of these battles taking place over the nature of the human being on Earth.

But there are signs that such knowledge is becoming available. To be sure, for most of us, all that I have said today about the struggle between luciferic and ahrimanic beings over the nature of humanity is hidden as if in a dim background to our existence. Yet these struggles do emerge into what we perceive quite clearly, what we know in full consciousness. And we have to learn to evaluate the first waves of the spiritual world as they break toward us—unless we want our whole civilization to be bathed in sleep.

These two battling camps, the luciferic in relationships of warmth and air, the ahrimanic in relationships of Earth and water, send their waves into our own cultural life. The luciferic camp today infects an outmoded theology, and we see its effects in the claims that Christ was merely a myth. For the Christ descended to Earth through the Mystery of Golgotha as a real being. Naturally, this is something that goes completely against the intentions of those beings who want to make us into moral automatons, who want to prevent our freedom. So they cross out the real being of Christ, calling Christ a myth. And you can follow this up in the literature of the nineteenth century, very cleverly put forward for example by David Friedrich Strauss, Kalthoff and their followers or imitators like Arthur Drews. They say Christ is a mythological figure, a mere image, the creation of human fantasy. Oh, much more will come from this camp! But this is the first, incoming wave.

The other wave, from the side of the ahrimanic host, offers the opposite view. There, Christ is put down, reduced to the "simple man of Nazareth." Jesus is taken for a mere physical personality—another theological hobbyhorse.

The transformation of Christ into a myth: purely luciferic. The transformation of He who underwent the Mystery of Golgotha into a mere human being, even if equipped with special characteristics: purely ahrimanic. This idea of Christ doesn't work at all. You have to ignore all the reports and traditions to come up with this "simple man of Nazareth." Yet in this theological hobbyhorse you can see the approach of the ahrimanic wave in human culture.

To evaluate these things properly, you have to be able to follow them up behind the scenes of normal earthly existence. Otherwise, if we can't be bothered to direct our gaze toward what can be said today from out of the spiritual world, then we will be able to judge such phenomena less and less well. As a result, they will take hold of us unconsciously. But it is becoming more and more dangerous for humanity to remain unconscious. Clear, bright, considerate examination of what is, a sense for the real—this is what we will need more and more.

And perhaps we can feel most strongly where this clarity, this sense for reality, will have to direct its gaze when we see the prevalence today of such remarkable phenomena as theology's denial of Christ on the one hand and making Him into a myth on the other. Such phenomena, which will become ever more widespread, show that we must attain clear and confident sight into the spiritual influences on the physical world, that is, on human beings, if these influences are not to corrupt humankind.

As I may have said once before, there were two men who found a molded piece of iron. One said, "A horseshoe! I'll put it on my horse." The other said, "No, it's a magnet, you can use it for something quite different." "I don't see any magnets," said the first, "You're crazy if you say there are invisible, magnetic forces in it. It's a horseshoe!"

This is the state of those who refuse to accept what can be said today from out of the spiritual world. They want to use the whole world as a horseshoe, because they can't admit the presence of super-sensible forces in it. They want to shoe their horses, instead of applying the magnetic power within it. Of course there was a time, not so long ago, when iron shaped that way was only good for shoeing horses. But today it's different.

A time will come when, even in normal social life with one another, human beings will need what the spiritual world has to say. We have to keep this in mind. Then anthroposophy will not merely go into our reason, which is of little value, but above all into our will. This does have significance. More and more, let us think of *that*.

CHAPTER FOUR

Understanding Sleep through Imagination, Inspiration and Intuition

For Steiner, it is an abdication of responsibility to speak of the "unconscious." Nothing is essentially unconscious—it is only outside awareness for the time being. Ultimately, we could be conscious of all that is and all that has been.

Sleep makes up an important category of what is outside normal awareness—after all, it occupies a third of our lives—and Steiner fully acknowledges that our everyday tools of thinking and feeling and so on are inadequate to penetrate the darkness of the night. He seeks in this lecture to give some details of how sleep appears when the higher perceptual functions he calls Imagination, Inspiration and Intuition begin to work.

Dreams do not initially offer an exact picture of what we experience on going to sleep. Only a heightened alertness that persists through sleep can behold, in full self-awareness, what takes place there. Then we can see, for example, the wave-like nature of ourselves and the world around us, a fluidity of consciousness that sets in during the early stages of sleep. At the same time, as Steiner describes in almost heart-wrenching terms, we have a longing for the divine that pulls us along through sleep and has an echo in waking life the next day.

Further reaches of sleep require still greater strength of soul if we are to experience them consciously. Steiner goes on to describe the soul's progressive immersion within the cosmos in sleep, and even to hint at the changes in the potential for experiencing sleep life that have come about since the time of Christ.

The immersion in the cosmos that we go through every night is the source of our impulses of initiative, but also our feelings and our insights, during the following day. We are nourished by sleep as by a time during which we spread ourselves out through immeasurable distances, receiving divine aid. We descend through the same stages once again as we wake up and locate ourselves in an earthly body in bed the next morning. The future progress of the planet depends on our bringing these nighttime experiences into waking consciousness.

STUTTGART, OCTOBER 9, 1922 GA 218

Today people tend to speak about forces within the soul that don't make their way into normal consciousness. On the other hand, people also admit their inability to examine such forces. The expression by which we encompass all this is "the unconscious." People like to speak about the "unconscious."

It is common to say that human awareness of the outer world depends on observation, experiment and reason. Yet in our own consciousness we find thoughts, feelings, impulses of will and so forth, and we become aware that in this life of the soul there are phenomena that cannot be investigated in their essential nature through the methods of outer science in the sense of experiment, observation and normal thinking. Nor is what we can survey through self-observation with the normal powers of consciousness adequate to penetrate to the essence of what arises in our inner life. And so we resort to talking about the "unconscious," and at the same time we give up on any attempt to penetrate directly into the world of this unconscious.

This renunciation is actually fully justified if we limit ourselves to the cognitive tools that are generally recognized today. For in fact with our normal cognitive means we can only conclude that during our waking life ideas, feelings, impulses of will—expressions of our nature—emerge within us, and that these seem to be bound to our external bodily nature. We cannot even say that what appears to be so dependent on our bodily state has any kind of existence beyond this bodily state.

Now you are aware that the anthroposophical view starts from this point, and takes seriously the fact that with the cognitive tools that are generally recognized today it is impossible to investigate the depths of the soul. We take seriously the fact that for these ordinary means, there is nothing to do but to speak of the "unconscious." In fact, we really don't need to look at the two boundaries of earthly life—birth and death. We need only look at the common, daily state of sleep, in order to be able to say that for real knowledge of the soul our normal ways of understanding cannot hold up to the following objection.

For these normal means of cognition, all our thinking, feeling and willing as they appear in everyday consciousness seem to depend so much on bodily states that we can well say they arise out of these bodily states as out of an Unconscious. During sleep, this merely organic life takes over completely, and doesn't allow ideas, feelings and will to emerge from it, so that there is nothing further we can say about it. At most we can say, based on the dreams that seem to come out of sleep and that are merely remembered in waking life, that the soul somehow continues during sleep—but it is all very shaky. At base, no serious, unprejudiced person with the ordinary cognitive tools of our time can do otherwise than to say that the phenomena of the soul appear to be dependent on our bodily state.

Precisely because anthroposophical understanding takes this ability or inability of normal cognitive means seriously, it strives to find other ways of knowing. As you know, we have often taken up such other means as Imagination, Inspiration and Intuition. Through these special kinds of understanding, which have to be developed by the individual through real effort, we can then strive for clarity about all that is left unclear through normal cognitive means. And today, without going over the portrayal I have often given of these three levels of cognition—imaginative, inspired and intuitive cognition—I would like to use them to portray something of the greatest importance with regard to human subconsciousness or unconsciousness, namely the life of the soul between falling asleep and waking up. I have often returned to this matter from various points of view, and I want to discuss it again today from one specific viewpoint. I want to simply portray the results of understanding sleep through Imagination, Inspiration and Intuition.

For normal consciousness, there is nothing to see as we fall asleep but the gradual loss of those contents that fill the soul during waking life. Then unconsciousness sets in. During waking life, within normal cognitive means, we cannot say what our soul is doing between the moment we fall asleep and the moment we wake up. Whatever might be going on psychologically in that state doesn't enter normal awareness. For normal consciousness, darkness spreads over whatever the soul might be experiencing, if it experiences anything at all during the state of sleep. But for Imaginative cognition sleep begins to grow light; the darkness begins to change into light, and we can reach conclusions about what the soul experiences at least during the first stages of sleep. Then inspired and intuitive cognition reach even further. You should not imagine that you then look into sleep the way you look into a display case. Rather, through imaginative, inspired and intuitive cognition you experience states of soul that are similar to sleep, with a relationship to the body that is similar to sleep. Yet now you are not experiencing this relationship unconsciously, but in a fully conscious state. And because during your waking life, in a fully awake state, you have experiences similar to those of sleep, you can also look directly into what the human soul accomplishes during sleep and even describe it.

As you go to sleep, the vague, unclear consciousness that arises can be permeated with dreams. This world of dreams is actually not much help, at first, in arriving at an understanding of the life of the soul. For what we can know with ordinary cognitive tools in daytime consciousness about dreams is something extremely external, and without a more developed cognitive ability, there is nothing reliable about our dreams. Anyone who really gets to know sleep also knows that dreams are more confusing than enlightening with regard to the state of sleep. The soul's journey between falling asleep and waking up is an unconscious one. To describe it out of imaginative, inspired and intuitive cognition, I have to describe it as if it were experienced consciously. The soul does experience these things, even though it knows nothing about them. They are present as facts, and as such they not only operate during sleep but have an effect above all on our physical organism that continues while we are awake. All day long, we carry with us the effects of our experiences in the previous night. And even if what we do in our consciousness is the most significant thing in our external lives, what really goes on in a human being depends very little on his or her consciousness but depends very greatly on what he or she experiences unconsciously between falling asleep and waking up again.

What we experience first of all, after our sense perceptions gradually become stilled and our impulses of will cease to work, is an undifferentiated state of soul. It is a generalized, indistinct experience, an experience where there is a definite sense of time, but the sense of space is almost completely extinguished. This experience can be compared with a kind of swimming, a kind of movement within a generalized, indistinct, universal substance. You really have to invent new words to express what the soul experiences here. I almost want to say that the soul experiences itself like a wave in a great ocean; like a wave that nevertheless feels inwardly organized, that feels surrounded on all sides by the rest of the sea, and that feels the effects of this sea within itself in the same way that during the day the impressions of colors or sounds or warmth are felt, perceived and thought about in distinct and differentiated ways. But during the day you feel yourself to be enclosed within your skin and located in a specific place. As you fall asleep, you feel like a wave in a generalized sea, now here, now there, and the definite feeling of location in space actually ceases. Again, I am saying "you feel" or "you experience," as if you were conscious; the fact is there, but without any awareness of it.

Nevertheless, your sense of time is still present in a general way. This experience is linked with another experience: abandonment. It is something like sinking into an abyss. Without any preparation, it would really be difficult consciously to experience even this first stage of sleep. You would really find it unbearable to lose almost all sense of space, to live only in a generalized experience of time, and to feel indistinctly enveloped in a vague sea with very little to distinguish, only that you are a self in a vague world. If you were conscious of it, you would feel as if you were hovering over an abyss. And connected with this is something like an incredible need in the soul for contact with the spirit; a terrible need to be connected with the spirit. And in the general sea you are swimming in, you have lost that feeling of certainty that comes with being connected to the material things of the waking world. And so you feel, or would feel if the situation were conscious, a deep longing for connection to the divine and the spiritual. You could also say that you actually experience this movement in an undifferentiated cosmic substance as the state of being hidden in God.

Please be aware of how I have to say these things. Again, I am representing it as if the soul experienced these things consciously. It is not experiencing them consciously, but you can well imagine that while you are experiencing things consciously during the day, a great deal takes place within your organism that is unconscious but is nonetheless a fact. Let us say, for example, that you experience joy. Your blood circulates differently during joy than during sorrow. You experience the joy or the sorrow consciously, but you don't experience the circulation of the blood in the one or the other state. Still, the blood's behavior is a fact. And there are real facts in our soul's life that correspond to what I have been describing as swimming in an undifferentiated world substance and as our deep need for God. Imaginative cognition does nothing other than to lift these facts into awareness, just as normal daytime consciousness lifts the blood's pulse into awareness as it changes in joy and sorrow. The facts are there, and the facts have an effect on waking life, so that when we wake up in the morning we are refreshed through the nighttime experience of our souls. What goes on in the soul by night, separated as it is from the body, has a significant effect on our waking life during the following day. We couldn't even use our body properly the next day if we hadn't lifted ourselves away from our connection with physical and sensory things and immersed ourselves in the experience of indefiniteness I have described. In waking life we have a need, emerging from the depths of our wills, to relate all that we find around us in a differentiated state to something universal. We have a need to relate the world of the senses to God. All this is an aftereffect of this first stage of sleep. We can ask: Why aren't human beings content with simply seeing the separate things of the world next to one another while awake? Why aren't we content to simply go through the world and accept the plants, the animals and so forth? Why do we begin to philosophize (which the simplest person does as much as the philosopher, and often understands much better than the philosopher)? Why do we ask how the individual things we see are grounded in something cosmic? We would never do all this if, during our sleep life, we were not livingly immersed in this realm without limits. Nor would we have a feeling for God if we didn't pass through just such a feeling during the first stage of sleep. We owe to sleep something extraordinarily significant in regard to the inward aspect of our human nature.

Now, as we go further in sleep we arrive at further stages that cannot be seen with Imaginative cognition, but for which Inspired cognition is necessary. What emerges there as the facts of our soul's experience, and then gets mirrored in Inspired consciousness, is a certain dispersion of the soul in an enormous number of separate entities, separate beings. The soul really splinters its life into many parts, and this splintering is connected to something that, when it lights up in awareness, appears as a kind of anxiety. After the soul has passed through the stage of hovering over the abyss or swimming in a universal cosmic substance, and felt a yearning for the divine and the spiritual, then it falls into a certain anxiety, or rather what would be anxiety if it were experienced consciously. It is basically the expression of the soul not merely swimming in a universal cosmic substance, but being immersed in individual soul-spiritual beings who have an existence with which the soul now comes into relationship. So the soul at this point is no longer a unity, but a multiplicity. And it is this multiplicity that is experienced as a certain anxiety. In some sense you have to move beyond this anxiety.

In the period of earthly evolution before the Mystery of Golgotha, the mystery centers put forth suggestions, in the form of the most varied spiritual exercises, and these found their way to the individual people. Through these exercises, people could experience feelings in addition to those stimulated by the external, sensory world, feelings evoked by the conceptions of God that were appropriate to those times. Then, humanity still felt, during waking life, that something of the spiritual world shone into consciousness. The further back we go in human evolution, the more we see that people had a kind of clairvoyance in very ancient times, and preserved vestiges of this clairvoyance into later times. They had a kind of inner vision of how, before we enter a life on Earth, we dwelt in a pre-earthly, spiritual existence as beings of soul and spirit. This was not a reasoned conclusion, or something people merely believed in. It was a certainty for them, since they experienced inwardly a remnant of a pre-earthly existence.

If I may be permitted a trivial analogy, I would say that if you inherit a certain fortune from your parents, then you know how this money has an effect on the course of your life. You know you did not earn it yourself, but it was handed down to you by your parents. In the same way, people in ancient times knew that certain experiences within their souls did not derive from what their eyes had seen, but were the inheritance of a pre-earthly existence. So it was easier for them to be directed by the leaders of the mystery sites as to how they should orient themselves in their feelings to the spiritual experiences within their souls.

Now, the strength they gained through the impulses that went forth from these mystery centers could be carried with them out of daytime life into their night life. It gave them the strength to be victorious, during sleep, through the period of anxiety I have described. For this anxiety does emerge from out of the depths of our sleep life. The strength to be able to carry over into the next day not a generalized exhaustion, but a refreshment of our whole organism that has to be acquired during the preceding day. So night and day are connected to one another. The night brings anxiety, at a certain stage of sleep, and the strength you have gathered out of a religious, spiritual experience on the previous day must be poured into this anxiety. When these two, the result of the previous day and the original experience of the night, become united, then they radiate out into the new life of the next day a refreshing strength for the whole organism.

It is inadequate for a real science of the spirit to speak in a general, abstract way about the presence of a universal divine order to the universe. It is not adequate to describe the things of the world only according to their sensory appearance and then say, "Well, there is a universal, cosmic order behind this sensory appearance." Spiritual science has to indicate very concretely how this divine cosmic order works. To meet the tasks of human evolution in the future, we cannot say simply that after a good sleep you feel refreshed and God supplies this refreshment. It would be all over with science if we had to keep to a strict scientificality for the sensory world, and couldn't extend this strictness to the supersensible. We must go further than the generalizing assertion that something like a divine order lies at the base of the world. We have to enter more and more into particulars; for example, how this anxiety at the second stage of sleep becomes intermingled with the strength drawn from the religious feeling of the previous day, which is still effective during the night, and out of this interaction there comes refreshment for the physical organism on the following day. This makes us more and more aware that what is really spiritual lives in what is really physical—even though, for the means of understanding considered valid today, physical content comes first, and then there are only general ways of talking about there being also something spiritual in or above this physical content. Yet human culture will deteriorate more and more unless we apply the same rigor we use in regarding the outer world to our investigations of the spiritual world. And if we do so, we notice through Inspired consciousness, as we pursue the stages of sleep from the first to the second, that the inner experience of the soul becomes something completely different from the experience of daily life.

Through natural science, too, if only we follow it through consistently, we can know that our inner life has something to do with the processes of breathing, the circulation of the blood and the process by which nourishment permeates our circulatory system. Something is happening, for instance, when we energetically move our bodies and so forth. Our souls and spirits are connected with bodily events, and if we talk about respiration or circulation, we know that we are talking about something that, during the day, involves our inner life.

The experience of our souls between falling asleep and waking up is *not* connected with the sensory realm, but it is also a very particular inner life that is related to something else, just as the inner life of the day can be related to the life of the breath or the life of our blood's circulation. Our inner life at night is connected with a certain development of forces that is comparable to the forces of breathing or circulation. The development of these forces is also comparable to an image of the planetary movements within our solar system. Notice that I do not say we pass through the movements of the planets themselves, but that we are connected to something that is an afterimage, a representation, a miniature of our solar system and its movements. Just as during the day we say that the white blood cells are circulating through us, the red blood cells are circulating through us, the breath circulates as we breathe in and out—in the same way we would have to say of our souls at night that the image of Mercury's movement is circulating within us, of Venus's movement, of Jupiter's. While we sleep, the life of our soul is a little cosmic solar system in miniature. Our life quits the sphere of what is personal and human and becomes something cosmic. Inspired cognition then finds the following process: When we are tired at night, the forces that kept the blood circulating during the day persist for a time through their own vitality in maintaining it. Later, however, for us to have a soul life during the day again, we need the impulse from our nightly experience of an image of the solar system. As we wake up, the aftereffect of what we experienced of these images of planetary movements is injected into us, implanted into us. It is this that links the cosmos with our individual life. If we didn't have the aftereffects of these nightly experiences, then as we awaken in the morning what we need in the way of forces could not stream into us so that consciousness could be present in the right way.

From all this you can already see how wrong it is that so many people today complain about insomnia. This is an extraordinarily strong self-deception. I can't go into it now, and those who are subject to this self-deception wouldn't believe it. They believe they really are not sleeping, while they are only in an abnormal sleep. They believe they are not outside their bodies, and not experiencing the existence of the planets. They are certainly in a dulled state, but it still permits them to experience what anyone experiences during a healthy sleep. Still, I cannot go into these exceptions right now.

In general, as I have said, we experience a cosmic life in this second stage of sleep. I hinted to you that in ancient times before the Mystery of Golgotha impulses went forth from the mystery sites through which people received the strength to move away from anxiety, to resist the disintegration and to go through what they had to go through in a healthy way. It was this strength that allowed people to arrive in the planetary spheres and not remain in the experience of disintegration. Anxiety came from the experience of disintegration; the experience of being in the planets came about through taking with them a certain strength from their experience of the previous day. Since the Mystery of Golgotha, human beings have had the possibility of achieving the same strength that previously came from the mystery centers by orienting themselves toward the events of this Mystery of Golgotha.

For anyone who actually lives through the Mystery of Golgotha within the soul in the right way, Christ becomes a strong leader at the moment the soul enters the realm of anxiety during sleep. In this way, modern humanity has, through the experience of Christ, what ancient humanity had through the mysteries.

From out of the stage of sleep that involves experience of the planetary solar system, we now enter the realm of the fixed stars. Having lived in the second stage of sleep in the image of planetary movement, we now live within the constellations of the fixed stars, above all in images of those stars that constitute the constellations of the zodiac. This experience of the constellations of the zodiac in the third stage of sleep is a very real one. There, too, we begin to sense the difference between the Sun as a planet and the Sun as a fixed star. It is not at all clear to modern human beings why the Sun counted in ancient astronomy both as a planet and as a fixed star. During the second stage of sleep, the Sun really has the qualities of a planet in our experience. We learn about its very special relationship to human experience on the Earth. Now, however, we get to know the Sun in its relationship to the other constellations of the zodiac. In short, we live within the cosmos in a still more intensive way than we did in the previous stage of sleep. We have the experience of the fixed stars, and from out of this experience of the fixed stars we receive still deeper, more meaningful impulses for our experience during the next day than any we could derive from merely planetary experience.

From our planetary experience we receive, if I may put it this way, a fire in our breathing and circulatory processes. But we need the effects of our experience of the fixed stars for this fire to really nourish the organism, for it to permeate the organism, which is apparently the most material thing but which is made of higher forces than the mere movement of the blood. As physical human beings we are dependent on our souls and spirits for the way in which particular materials circulate within us. All this is connected, if I may say so, with the highest heavens. It is connected with our feeling, in the third stage of sleep, that images of the constellations of fixed stars are within us, just as we feel our stomach or lungs within us during the day while we are awake. During the day our body is inwardly in motion, filled up with the movements of the breath and blood. In the same way, at night, our soul, our substance within the soul, is something that possesses the images of the planetary motions within it. And just as during the day we have stomach, lungs and heart within us, so during the night we have the constellations of the fixed stars. They are our "insides" at night. So during the state of sleep we really become cosmic beings. This third stage of sleep is the deepest; from it we gradually return to waking day once more. Why do we return? We would not go back into waking life if certain forces in our souls did not take effect to lead us back into our physical organisms.

Now, I have described to you from the most varied standpoints how we can refer to these forces. Today, I would like to portray them from a cosmic standpoint. If you get to know the experience of the fixed stars, you also realize that the forces drawing us back into our physical organism are the forces of the Moon. That is, they are that which corresponds, in the spirit, to what appears, as a physical image, as the Moon. Naturally this isn't a question of whether it is currently the full Moon or something like that. Rather, spiritually speaking, the Moon can even shine right through the Earth. It does have something to do with the metamorphoses that the Moon's visibility expresses, but this would lead us into much finer distinctions than I can address today. In general, then, it is the Moon forces that lead us back. Just as we are always permeated by the planetary forces during sleep, and by the forces revealed in the constellations of the fixed stars, and remain permeated by them (for they have their after-effects during the following day), so too we are permeated continually by what in the cosmos corresponds to the physical Moon as spiritual forces. And it is these Moon forces that draw us back. In reality, it is an extraordinarily complex process. To describe it at all I would have to say that just as a rubber band is stretched to a certain point and then it snaps back, so we stretch out the Moon forces, in a sense, up to a point from which we have to return. We reach this point in the third stage of sleep, and we are drawn back, step by step, through these Moon forces that are so inwardly bound up with the influx of the soul and spirit, into the physical world: from the third stage to the second, from the second to the first.

You see, everything we can carry in the way of forces of initiative in our mental life and our feeling life during the day is an after-effect of the experience of the fixed stars during the night. Everything we carry in the way of wisdom, cleverness, is the result of the planetary experience. But what radiates into daily life from out of our nighttime experience in the cosmos has to come by way of the detour of the body. The experience of the fixed stars shoots into our daily life by the detour of the transformation of our foods. Foods would not arrive in the brain in such a way as to enable the forces of initiative to develop if this whole process were not ignited by what we experience in the night through the fixed stars. And we could not think reasonably if the circulation of our breath and blood did not receive by the day the aftereffects of our planetary experience during the previous night.

Such things can only be described in general terms, and their apparent absence in people who suffer from insomnia does give us the task of explaining the abnormal circumstances they encounter. Thoroughly understood, they do not actually contradict these truths. But these truths, correct as they are in a general way, do give us the only possibility of really explaining the essence of what happens in any individual case.

Real understanding of human nature is only possible if we are conscious in the deepest sense of the fact that we do not live only within our physical body inside our skin; rather, we live in the whole world. Our life within the whole world is only hidden from normal consciousness because this consciousness has been weakened for the sake of daytime experience. It is at most in our sense of light that we experience again something of our participation in the being of a universal cosmos. Perhaps in other feelings too, but in very muted ones, we have some sense of feeling *inside* the cosmos while awake. But everything given to us in this way grows silent so that we may develop an individual consciousness between waking and falling asleep again. It is so that we will not be distracted by all that plays into our experience from out of the cosmos. During the night it is just the reverse. There our experience is cosmic, or the image of a cosmic experience, but a faithful image, as I have suggested. There we really do have a cosmic experience, and because we have to go through this cosmic life, our daytime consciousness is dampened, weakened.

The future evolution of humanity will consist in our living our way ever more and more into the cosmos, so that we will someday bring about the era in which we will feel ourselves within the Sun, Moon and stars just as now we feel we are on the Earth with our consciousness. Then we will look from the cosmos onto the Earth, just as now we look from the Earth into the cosmos in our current waking state. But the way in which we do our looking will be fundamentally different.

Anyone who really has evolution in mind will be aware that human consciousness itself is subject to evolution, and that the bodily consciousness we have in our current stage is only a transitional stage to another consciousness. This other consciousness is nothing but the reflection, in the soul, of facts that we experience already, every night. We need them, because in their aftereffects these facts really carry our daily life. Our further evolution will consist in being aware, during normal life, of what is unconscious for us today. But for this it is necessary for people to find their way into spiritual science. Just as you need a direction if you are going to swim anywhere, the ordinary consciousness of today needs a direction. We cannot simply let ourselves be carried, as in normal cognition. It is only spiritual science that can give this direction, because it reveals (as far as we need for today) what already lives within the human being but in today's human being is not yet conscious. We have to bring it into our awareness, or we will make no real cosmic progress.

CHAPTER FIVE

An Active Spirit:
Dreams and the Spiritual Researcher

〰〰〰

KNOWLEDGE OF THE higher worlds isn't easy. Steiner continually attempts to raise our standards, to assert that we cannot go about knowing spiritual circumstances with the same kind of knowing we normally use in the physical world. Here he makes it all the harder, emphasizing three special characteristics of higher knowledge.

First, ordinary memory cannot capture these experiences, for ordinary memory works with sensory images, and there are no such images in the spiritual world itself. Second, though practice makes perfect in earthly capacities, repeated spiritual experience is more difficult each time. Finally, spiritual events happen with an instantaneous rapidity—actually outside of time—so that to grasp them at all requires immense presence of mind.

All three of these characteristics have to do with immediacy. Spiritual experience cannot be captured—through memory, practice, or normal mental rapidity—since the spirit happens in a timeless now, the nunc stans of Augustine, and there is no fixed information to be known about it.

69

This lecture represents one of Steiner's frankest, most approachable explorations of just how difficult spiritual experience is, and how different from what normally passes through our minds. He is clearly describing processes in which he has great expertise, and which he approaches with a modernity that seems to leap off the page into our own day.

As elsewhere, Steiner here emphasizes the symbolic nature of dreams, and recounts examples of the sense-stimulus type where outer events, or the health of the dreamer, influence the dream. But he goes on to suggest that the dream as dreamt is a poor substitute, a substitute clothed in images of waking life, that stands in for a living, spiritual reality that originally is free of such images. The dream therefore presents a "challenge" that Steiner more or less dares us to take up. Dreams challenge us to awaken to the spiritual world behind dreams—a world of beings and meanings that is not just more convincing and self-evident than the dreams as they are normally remembered, but also more so than our daytime, sense-perceptible reality.

———

BERLIN, MARCH 21, 1918 GA 67

A true understanding of reality serves human life. Anyone who realizes this, anyone who has woken up to it, also wants to know about the aspects of human life covered by spiritual science. Yet the kind of effort required may be uncomfortable, and spiritual science has to point out again and again that the powers of understanding adequate to normal and even scientific life cannot provide entry into spiritual life. We find it uncomfortable to have to discover new sources of understanding. If you really consider spiritual science without prejudice, though, you will find that ordinary, healthy human understanding is capable of insight into all that spiritual science offers. Yet people prefer not to apply healthy human understanding to spiritual science. They do not want to get involved in anything that would require the soul to develop.

The facts of spiritual science can only be *researched* by the spiritual scientific methods described here and elsewhere. Once the facts have been researched, however, they can certainly be grasped by the healthy human understanding and through ordinary life experience. Still, we have that inner cognitive laziness. We shy back from spiritual science and turn instead to other sources closer to contemporary natural science, to the laboratory, to the dissection room. So those who cannot bring themselves to work in the sense of spiritual science often appeal to abnormal phenomena in human life, which can be observed in the external world, in order to glimpse certain aspects of spiritual life. For they imagine they can solve certain riddles of existence through the abnormal element in human beings. So spiritual science has widely been confused with efforts to understand the spirit by looking into all kinds of abnormal limit-experiences in human life.

For this reason, it will be necessary for me to consider these limit-experiences. Their very abnormality does hint at certain secrets of existence, but they can only really be understood through spiritual science. Without this help, they will lead to innumerable errors as to the true reality of spiritual life. The area I want to look at today is more or less well known to everyone, in all its breadth and fascination and difficulty, since it relates to certain correspondences between outer life and the hidden underpinnings of our existence. I am talking about dreams.

Proceeding from dream life, I will then be considering other limit-experiences in human existence through which the view could arise that they are somehow especially close to the underpinnings of life. These are the phenomena of hallucination, visionaries, somnambulism and mediums—to the extent these can be addressed in a brief lecture.

Anyone who wants to understand these areas from the view-point of spiritual science must keep in view the particular aspects of real spiritual research that can throw light on these subjects. So I would like to re-emphasize a few points of what I have said in earlier lectures that can make an appropriate basis for the discussion of these phenomena. Spiritual science has to be based on the real development of forces within the human soul that are hidden within ordinary consciousness, as well as in the consciousness by which ordinary science works. I have indicated before that the human soul is in a position to draw forth slumbering forces within itself through exercises of a purely inward nature, that have nothing to do with the body. In this way, the soul acquires the capacity to look directly into the real life of the spirit. I will have to characterize here the most essential precondition for the soul to make itself independent of the body in this kind of supersensible cognition. Above all, we have to keep in mind something I have said before and will now repeat in brief.

I have said that our stance with regard to spiritual reality has to be different from our stance toward external, physical, sensory reality. Above all, what we experience as body-free souls in the spiritual world cannot immediately transfer itself into memory like a normal experience. What we experience in the spirit has to be continually experienced afresh, just as an external physical reality, if you want not merely to remember it but to have it in front of you, has to be in front of you again each time. We cannot capture real spiritual experience by the same kinds of mental representations as those by which we remember the ordinary representaions of everyday life. Anyone who thinks we can simply doesn't know what real spirituality is. If we nonetheless seem to remember spiritual experiences (which is certainly possible), this is because we bring them into ordinary consciousness, in the same way we can do with our views of external, physical reality. Still, we have to distinguish between this remembering of one's own self-formed mental pictures and the immediate experience of a spiritual process, the immediate encounter with a spiritual being. So this is one special characteristic of body-free experience—that it does not enter memory directly.

Another characteristic (also already mentioned by me), is that in other areas of human exercise and practice, continual exercise makes it easier and easier to accomplish what is practiced. With spiritual cognition, strangely enough, the reverse is the case. The more often you have the same spiritual experience, the harder it is for the soul to put itself in such a state as to have this spiritual experience again in the same way. You have to learn the method for repeating a spiritual experience, since it cannot be renewed twice in the same way.

The third characteristic is that real spiritual experiences sweep through the soul so rapidly that it takes presence of mind to grab hold of them. Otherwise the event sweeps past so quickly that it is already over by the time the attention is directed toward it. As I have said, you have to practice mastering those situations in life in which you cannot consider and dilly-dally for a long time over a decision but must act quickly and decisively. This kind of presence of mind is necessary to really bring spiritual experiences into the zone of our attentiveness.

I mention these peculiarities of spiritual life because they show how very different experience in the spirit is from experience in the outer physical sense world, and how little it is justifiable when those who know nothing about it claim that it is only ideas and concepts from the external sense world that the spiritual researcher transfers into some dreamed-up spiritual world. Anyone who really knows about the special characteristics of the spiritual world also knows that it is very different from the ordinary sense world. Nothing can be transferred there from the sense world. Instead, the soul needs to develop special capacities to meet spirit as spirit.

Still more must be fulfilled in the soul of those who want to do spiritual research. The first condition is that the soul must be exposed as little as possible to the peculiar condition we can call passivity. Those who particularly love to go through life in a dream, to make themselves passive and allow the revelations of spiritual reality to flow into them in a dreamy, mystical mood, are ill equipped to really enter the spiritual world. Let us be clear about this: in the realm of actual spiritual life, the Lord does not give himself to his own in sleep! On the contrary, what makes us specially apt to enter the spiritual world is an active spirit, a certain eagerness in the pursuit of real thoughts and in the linkage among diverse thoughts. It is a certain speedy grasp of the connections among thoughts, a certain love for inner spiritual activity. The capacity to be a medium and the capacity for real spiritual understanding are as different as night and day. This condition really has to be met if true spiritual research is to occur.

Another condition is that the soul of a real spiritual researcher has to be free from all suggestibility. Your soul has to be as skeptical as possible, confronting the things of external life as critically as possible. Anyone who loves to be told by others what to do in life, who disowns his or her own capacity to judge and decide freely, is poorly suited to be a spiritual researcher. If you know how common suggestibility is even in normal life, you also know how hard it is to combat it. We need only consider how common suggestibility is in public life, how little people try to make their souls fit for independent judgment, how little they make their affairs reflect their own wills. Those who become involved in spiritual research to achieve a relationship with the spiritual world based on their healthy human understanding must often meet with the reproach that they are engaged in blind faith. But a spiritual researcher who really tries to penetrate into the spiritual world through a contemplative consciousness will never want such blind followers. A society that merely followed such a spiritual researcher would be a caricature of a society fit to develop spiritual understanding. On the contrary, the real spiritual researcher will recognize with joy that precisely those closest to him or her eventually arrive at an independent judgment, a certain inner freedom. They are not attached to the spiritual researcher through blind discipleship, nor through suggestibility, but through a common interest in the spiritual world.

I want to mention one further quality that can shed light on the relationship of spiritual reality to physical reality, on the relationship of the human soul to this spiritual world. It is often said that the spiritual researcher merely brings prejudices from the physical world to a spiritual world he or she "dreams up." But if you really enter the spiritual world, what happens is always something quite different. You find out that whatever brought you into the spiritual world, whatever guides your experiences there, is always completely different from what you thought beforehand. Precisely through this difference, you see that you are dealing with a world you only enter by making your soul suitable to it, and that you are not carrying memories of the physical world into a dreamed-up world.

And there is something more, which may sound paradoxical but is nevertheless learned through decades of experience in regard to the things of the spiritual world. You may be very well schooled in body-free cognition; you may be very well practiced in beholding the spiritual world—yet if you want to see once again a particular being or process, especially involving the connection of the spiritual to the physical, you often find that your first spiritual experience, your first feeling that you know some truth about something in the spiritual world, was false. So it is good for the spiritual researcher to acquire a kind of caution, aware that the first experience may be false.

Further experience shows what is right and what is false, and how to compare them. So as a rule the spiritual researcher will be slow to communicate results, knowing how necesssary it is in the realm of spiritual life to win through to the truth through illusion and error. This illusion, this error, are there because we research spiritual life by proceeding from out of the sensory world. We bring the power of judgment and the style of seeing from the sensory into the spiritual world. At first, we always tend to apply what we bring over in this way to the spiritual world. This is how the false judgments come about. Just through this process of having to convince yourself anew each time that you have to relate differently to spiritual and physical things, you come to know the various intimate peculiarities of spiritual experience.

We could bring in other examples, but this is enough to show that spiritual experience always seems like something paradoxical in comparison with ordinary, everyday experience. The eternal, the imperishable element in the human soul, cannot express itself for the ordinary, body-bound consciousness. It is hidden, for here in physical life through our bodily organization we can only know physicality. This is why it is so important for the spiritual researcher to strictly emphasize that cognition of the spiritual takes place outside the body. The moment the body participates in the acquisition of such cognition it becomes false. It also becomes false when body-bound memory becomes involved.

Another result of immediate experience of the spirit is the knowledge that anyone who gives up his or her free will, who comes under any kind of compulsion or suggestion, is immediately excluded from the spiritual world to which the eternal part of the soul belongs. This applies to any bodily action, including speech, that is not transmitted by one's own will. Hence, a fundamental condition for experience in the spiritual world is that the body must not participate in this cognition. The other fundamental condition is that one must try to ensure that everything carried out by the body comes from the capacity for judgment and the decisions of free will.

These preconditions offer the basis for our consideration of abnormal regions of soul life. In real cognition of the spirit there is a revelation of what is normally unconscious for us; it can enlighten us about the eternal, and truly free, essence of our soul. We can then compare it to what comes to light through the abnormal phenomena of the soul.

We cannot quite count as "abnormal" what meets us, or beats against us, in the rising and falling waves of dreamlife. This dreamworld has already become the object of natural scientific and philosophical investigations. Yet we cannot say the methods that have proved so brilliant for external natural science are particularly suited to penetrate into this boundary phenomenon of human life. Here, too, reliance on the methods of natural science will not help us penetrate to the truth of the matter. Despite a sense of being independent of authority, there is a strong predilection, in our time, to subject oneself to authority in certain circumstances. If someone is considered a great figure in public life and publishes a fat book about research into abnormal mental phenomena, then many who don't quite understand the matter will praise the book. And our "authority-free" society will assume that the book is something substantial.

I would like to select one book from among the philosophical treatments of dreamlife, written by a brilliant German scholar, Johannes Volkelt, currently Professor of Philosophy and Pedagogy in Leipzig. He wrote it in 1875 on the subject of dream fantasy, when he was not yet a professor. This very valuable book still haunts him, and is probably the reason why he remains merely an assistant professor. The extraordinarily significant Swabian aesthetician, Friedrich Theodor Vischer, wrote a fine treatise on this book. It is only the recent, reigning academic prejudices, with their mistaken view of science, that have failed to take up what this book initiated (however meagerly), and instead have buried it under the common prejudices that prevent us from really penetrating dreamlife.

Of course, in the short space available here, I can only sketch out a description, but I want to do so in such a way as to illuminate things from a spiritual scientific viewpoint. Everyone knows dreamlife, with its rising and falling waves of mental pictures, and everyone knows about the external peculiarities of dreamlife. I only want to characterize a few of these in more detail.

We can notice that dreams arrive in response to certain circumstances. Dreams of this kind include the so-called "sense-stimulus dreams." You need only recall how a dream can come about when you sleep near a grandfather clock. Under certain conditions, the motion of the clock's pendulum can become the tramping of horses or something similar. So you develop certain symbols in a dream. I want particularly to emphasize this since dream experience can derive from numerous external sense impressions. But whatever is acting on the outer senses never acts the same way in the dream as it does in normal waking consciousness. There is always a transformation of the sense impression into a symbol, into something the life of the soul has transformed.

Such dreams are widely known. Johannes Volkelt recounts the following story. A teacher dreams he is teaching his class. He is waiting for a student to answer a question he has posed with the word "yes." But instead of "yes" the student answers "yo," which is unpleasant for the teacher. He repeats the question, and the student answers not "yo" but "ho." Then the whole class starts to cry, "Fire-ho." The teacher wakes up and outside the firetruck is driving past and someone is crying "Fire-ho!" This last impression on the senses gave rise to the whole complicated affair of the dream.

Another example, also from Volkelt (as far as possible I want to draw on examples already in the literature) goes as follows. A Swabian woman visits her sister in a bigger city. The sister is the wife of a minister. Both sisters listen to the sermon. The minister is beginning it very nicely. But then suddenly he grows wings and begins to crow like a rooster. One sister says to the other, "Now, that's a funny way to preach." The sister answers in the dream, "But that's how the synod has ordered them to preach now." The wife wakes up and outside she hears a rooster crowing. So the rooster's cry, which otherwise would enter awareness as a dry, sober sound, has been transformed in the soul. Everything else clustered around the rooster's cry. This is the nature of the sense-stimulus dream.

But dreams can also come about through internal stimuli, and once again it is not the stimulus as such that makes its appearance, but a symbol transformed by the soul. Someone dreams about a hot, steaming oven; he wakes up and finds his heart was beating fast. Flying dreams, which are very common, generally come from abnormal conditions of the lungs during sleep. And so on. We could list hundreds of such examples. Indeed, the simple enumeration of the different kinds of dreams could be greatly extended. Though we cannot fully engage with all the deeper aspects of the matter, I would like to mention a few.

The literature on dreams has not been especially fortunate in discovering what is actually taking place in the soul when external events are transformed into symbols. But this question is more interesting than all the others. What is it in the soul that can link an external event, or a memory welling up from the darkness of sleep, to such very different images in the dream? For whatever it is that allows us, in normal daily life, to connect one impression to the next based on our experiences, is *not* the active element in dreams. I could offer you hundreds of example of what I mean here, but one will have to suffice. A woman dreams that she has to cook for her husband, which can be hard duty at times. In her dream, she has already offered him many suggestions. To her first, she gets the response, "I don't like it." To the second, "I don't like it." To the third, "I really don't like that. Forget about it!" And so on. The woman is very unhappy about this in the dream. Then she thinks, "Well, we have a salted grandmother in the basement. She's a bit tough, but why don't I cook her for tomorrow?" This is another dream you can find in the literature. Anyone who knows dreams will not doubt that the dream really took this course. It is not a rare kind of dream. Our first impression is that the mood of anxiety permeates the dream. Something has happened that makes the woman anxious. This mood, which need have nothing to do with the image of cooking and so forth, has transformed itself into such images. They are simply a variation on the theme of anxiety. To emerge from anxiety in the dream, the soul needs such metamorphoses. The idea of the salted grandmother is humorous, and the soul uses it as a means to overcome anxiety in a grotesquely comical way, to shift into an ironic, humorous mood. This is something you can always notice in dreams. There is an oscillation, a back-and-forth movement, as with a clock's pendulum, between moods—between tension and release, between anxiety and humor, and so forth. The articulation of dream images depends on the person's predominant feelings at the moment. On this view, the dream is formed in order to overcome certain tensions in the soul. From out of the necessity to change tension into release, and release into tension, there is born the (often insignificant) image within the dream. The soul conjures up something to serve as an image of what is really going on.

If we take into account the whole breadth of dreamlife, two special features are particularly noticeable. The first is that what we call "logic" in normal life is silent during dreams. The dream has a different, non-logical way of moving from one object to the next. Of course, you may object that some dreams are in fact very logical. But this is only apparently the case. If you really look closely, you see it is not so. When you have dream images that follow one another in logical sequence, it is not because you provide such log-

ical sequence during the dream itself, but because you put together
mental pictures that you had already assembled logically in daily
life, or that for some other reason hang together logically on their
own. The logic here is a kind of memory imported into the dream,
while the dream actions themselves don't proceed along logical
lines at all. You can always discover that a deeper, more intimate
element of the soul lies behind dream actions. To take one true
example, someone dreams that he has to meet a friend and knows
this friend will scold him for something. He dreams that he arrives
at his friend's door. In that moment, though, the whole situation
changes. When he walks in, he enters a cellar filled with wild beasts
who want to eat him up. It occurs to him that he has a lot of needles at home, and that these needles can spray a poison that can kill
the animals. Then they turn into a pack of young dogs, and he
wants only to stroke them very gently. This dream, which offers a
typical dream sequence, once again shows a tension called forth by
a kind of fear, occasioned by the friend, which expressed itself in the
wild animals and achieved release through the soul's invention of
changing the wild, fearful beasts into lovable young dogs. You see
that the process is not logical.

The following kind of dream often comes about as well. You
have worked hard to find the solution to some problem just before
going to bed, yet you couldn't find it. Then you have a dream and
in the dream you find the solution, so that you can actually write
it down in the morning. Such things do happen. But if you don't
investigate them properly, you will misunderstand them. You
should not imagine that you did in fact find the real solution
through the dream. What you really found in the dream, and what
you imagine you are remembering, was something completely different. It wasn't necessarily logical at all; instead, it could just be a
case of tension and release. Before falling asleep, you were in a
state of emotional tension, so you couldn't solve the problem. You

struggled and worried, but something was missing. Through dreaming, you became healthy, and so on waking you could solve the problem.

Moral judgment is also missing during our dreams. In a dream you may commit all kinds of crimes you would be ashamed of during the day. The objection could be made that it is precisely during dreams that conscience becomes active, and comes to the fore in a special way. We need only recall the dreams mentioned in Shakespeare's plays. Writers quite rightly point to the apparent capacity of dreams to cast moral reproaches on the dreamer. This is based on an inexact observation, however. Rather, during dreams we are torn away from the kind of normal moral judgments we acquire through interaction with others. If the dream still seems to portray moral prejudices and reproaches, this is because we have a certain mood of satisfaction when we behave morally; we are happy to be able to affirm something morally. It is this satisfaction, rather than the moral judgment, that appears to us in the dream. Moral judgment is just as absent from dreams as logic. If you really want the truth, you have to go about it more exactly and initimately than in normal life or even science. Such matters do not reveal themselves to our normal, heavy-handed methods. It is actually very important that neither morality nor logic find their way into the dreamworld, and we shall soon see why.

I would like now to put forward another quality of dreams that, through even the most external look at dreams, can suggest to us the relationship between the soul and the world during dreaming. Of course, this relationship can only be fully explained when it is investigated from a spiritual-scientific viewpoint. But even someone who looks at a dreamer externally can say that in sleep, the human being is closed off both from his or her own life and from whatever is happening in the surrounding environment. Spiritual science goes on to show that in sleep we enter the spiritual world as beings of soul and spirit, and we are reconnected with the body at the moment of waking up. But we can leave this aside for the moment and only call to mind what is evident to ordinary consciousness. In sleep, we are closed off both from the environment and also from everything that our own bodies normally offer to our awareness. While dreaming, images surge up and down, but this does not change our relationship to the environment. The images are formed in such a way that this relationship holds steady. Our normal experience of the environment, the sober engagement with external impressions, cannot find its way into our dreams. Impressions may come, as we have seen. But the characteristic way in which our senses respond to these impressions is absent. The soul replaces the normal sober impression with a symbol. So the relationship to the external world remains closed off.

We could confirm this with countless examples. Even what arises from our own bodily nature comes to expression differently than during our normal, waking-life relationship to our body. For instance, if the covers are too warm and so your feet grow too warm, in the normal waking state you would feel that your feet are too warm. In the dream, by contrast, you imagine that you are walking over hot coals or something similar. Again, the main thing is the symbolic transformation achieved by the soul.

As much as we may try to investigate dreams through the means of external science, we cannot do so simply because there is nothing to which we can compare a dream. Dreams really enter the normal world as a kind of miracle; they cannot be compared to anything else. That is the essential point. It is only the spiritual scientist who can compare the dream with something else. Why? Because of a personal familiarity with what we find when we enter the spiritual world. There, we can percieve that normal logic, applicable to external, sensory life, is inadequate. Anyone who rises to the spiritual world has to be able to express experiences in the spiritual world in the form of symbols. This is why the first stage of cognition of the spiritual world is called "imaginative cognition." You know that these symbols are not realities, but you also know that they express realities. Of course, such symbols have to be formed from out of the true laws arising from the spirit; they must not come from arbitrary fantasy. The spiritual researcher comes to know how, quite apart from the physical-sensory world, you can connect various mental pictures and make symbols. This first state of spiritual cognition can be compared with the unconscious activity of dreams. Here is a basis for comparison, and also something more.

Those who really make progress in understanding the spiritual world gradually find that their own dreams undergo a change. They become more regular. From out of confused images, like the salted grandmother, there gradually come others that express something meaningful; the whole dreamlife becomes permeated by meaning. So the spiritual researcher gets to know the special family resemblance between the life of dreams and the life sought through spiritual research. It is in this way that we can say what it really is in the soul that dreams. We come to know the state of the soul during Imagination. In this state, you know you are standing within the spiritual world. If you know this quality of soul, this orientation of the soul, then you can compare it with the orientation of the soul during sleep. From out of this conscientious comparison, you can determine that what dreams within the soul, what is really active in the soul when a person lets the chaotic dream events play out, is actually the spiritual, eternal core of a human being. As dreamers we participate in the world to which we belong as beings of soul and spirit.

This is one result. I would like to characterize another result through a personal experience of mine. Not long ago, I held a lecture in Zurich about dreaming and related matters. Afterward, I heard that some of my listeners, who felt particularly clever because of their analytic psychology, or psychoanalysis, said, "This fellow is caught up in views we in psychoanalysis have long since outgrown. He thinks dreams are real. We know that dreams are only to be understood as symbolic representations of the soul." I don't want to go into the whole subject of psychoanalysis here, but only mention that this cleverness is based on a clumsy misunderstanding. It would never occur to a real spiritual researcher to take what appears in a dream as immediately real in just the way it appears in the dream. Nor would such a researcher take the course of the dream as directly symbolic after the fashion of the psychoanalyst. Spiritual research depends on something entirely different.

Anyone who knows dreams knows that ten people can report the most varied dreams, and yet the same facts can lie behind them all. One recalls that he climbed a mountain and was happily surprised at the summit; another tells of how she went through a dark tunnel to a door that unexpectedly opened; a third has a completely different story. The dreams don't seem to follow anything like the same course, yet they could refer to a similar real experience, a similar tension and release that finds symbolic expression in different images at different times. So it is not a question of the reality of the dream, nor even, as the psychoanalysts think, a matter of the symbols; rather, what counts is the inner dramatic movement of the dream. One must be in a position to understand, based on a sequence of meaningless images, the inner drama, the reality, in which the dreaming soul's spiritual essence is living.

This spiritual reality is something altogether different from what finds expression in the dream images. This is what counts. So the dream points the way deep into the subconscious and unconscious foundations of the soul. But what it bodies forth is only a disguise for what is actually, really being experienced while dreams are being dreamt.

As always, I must emphasize that I really don't want to revive ancient prejudices in any area. I am not speaking out of presuppositions borrowed from medieval or Asian so-called spiritual science. You can find this kind of thing in Blavatsky and in others who draw from all sorts of dark sources. Everything said here can stand up to natural scientific judgment, which could even be useful on occasion. Spiritual science is offered in the full consciousness that we live in a natural scientific age, with full awareness of what natural science has to say about existence and its riddles, but also in full awareness of what it cannot say about the spiritual side of life.

Now, where do the images of a dream sequence come from? If you really are standing in the midst of spiritual experience, free from the body, then you have the spiritual world before you with all the processes and beings within it. If you are dreaming, your consciousness is not awake enough to have the full spiritual world before you. Instead, the soul steps in with its memories of ordinary life, and so the dream arises as the soul makes contact with the bodily nature. The dream is not experienced in the body, but it is caused by contact between the soul and the body. This is why the experiencer of the dream beholds things from the ordinary course of life, but grouped together so as to express those inner tendencies of which I have spoken. To characterize what the dream really is, you could say it is an experience of the individual soul-spiritual essence of the human being. But what is experienced is not the eternal, but the temporal. The eternal is the conscious, active element in the dream. Yet what transmits this activity is transitory, ephemeral. So the key point is this: the eternal is experienced in the dream precisely as the temporal, the transitory, the normal content of life.

With this I have presented, though in a sketchy way, the essence of the dream in the light of spiritual science. We have seen why the dream's content does not really express what is really taking place in the soul—where tension follows release, and release follows tension. That is the soul in the world of the eternal, the soul in a body-free element. What becomes conscious as a transformation of this experience derives from the connection with the circumstances of ordinary life.

To summarize what we have said today: It is certain that the abnormal experiences of life [dreaming, hallucinations, art] lead us into the spiritual realm. For it is the spiritual world that casts its light into our lives, even if we experience it in an abnormal way. But we should not try to reproduce these abnormal states artificially for the sake of knowing something, any more than we should reproduce sickness artificially. What is it that remains behind, after all such phenomena, like a living challenge? Just this: that people *want* to find the way into true experience of the spirit. And there remains the noteworthy finding that, through spiritual science, we can defend dreams against the suspicion that they have something to do with the experiences of sickness—though there are, of course, connections between the two.

Dreams challenge us to find our way into the true spiritual world, and when we see this it becomes deeply significant to examine this seemingly chaotic world of dreams. A dream, with its strange images, is an important cosmic riddle knocking on our door, illogical and amoral but a clear hint of the spiritual world itself. Then we can affirm what the brilliant aesthetician and philosopher Vischer said about Volkelt's book: when we look at the dream with its rich poverty, with its poor wealth, with its ingenious stupidity, with its dumb genius, and consider its unconscious creativity, then we will recognize that it does after all point to what is spiritually active in humanity, and can be sought. And Vischer is right when he goes on to say, "Anyone who thinks this spiritual realm of the dream isn't worthy to be made the object of true research only shows that he doesn't have much spirit himself." But if the world of dreams challenges us to approach the spiritual world, spiritual science wants to actually meet this challenge. The dream can only attain to images of the past, even if the soul is present for this process with its eternal essence. Through spiritual cognition, the soul that lives in the eternal world can also fill itself with images that express the spiritual reality corresponding to its own primal nature. And just as the soul finds its rightful place in the sensory world through the senses, it also finds its rightful place in the reality of soul and spirit as a being of soul and spirit.

CHAPTER SIX

Our Inner Undercurrent:
A Continual Dreaming

OUR THOUGHTS NEVER *cease. We have one event in our minds after the other, never standing still, always opting for quantity over quality. It is as if our minds had made a Faustian bargain with the devil, vowing never to rest in the moment. Many of the thoughts in a day are mere repetitions of our favorite worries, but none of them ever lasts for long at a stretch. Emerson said, "Thought is the manna that cannot be stored." Even in the debased form of everyday consciousness, the inner world is a world of continual change.*

Steiner challenges us to notice this quality and to relate it to the sea of thoughts and images we emerge from on waking up each morning. He wants us to observe the fabric of our minds far more closely than we usually do, so as to notice the thoughts and images that disappear at the mind's horizon every instant. He wants our attention to become so fine-grained it even becomes aware, alongside this stream of consciousness, of the stream of un-consciousness: of how our nighttime dreaming, with its fluidity and variety, continues throughout the day, only drowned out by sensory impressions as starlight is drowned out by the Sun.

For at night we are not, as during the day, locked up inside our bodies. Our going "out" into the spiritual world is also a merging with the world we normally perceive as physical during the day. The world we see as outside in normal consciousness is experienced as within us during spiritual or nighttime consciousness. And this outer world is a world of thoughts and beings. We lose our separateness and merge with the unified world.

Among the spiritual processes we may have access to in the night, Steiner includes the very "physical body" we have supposedly left behind. For now we perceive the inner being of the body's organs—heart, liver, lungs and so on—just as we merge with the meaning-essence of all the supposedly physical and outer world. During the day, we actually experience our bodies in a most limited fashion. We never see them objectively, never merge with them as aspects of the world of sacred thought. And so, rather than see the body's organs as only functional elements of the normally-perceived physical body as it operates during waking life, Steiner understands them to embody vast, even cosmic forces whose operation outlasts our stay on Earth—even the Earth itself.

Toward the end of the lecture, Steiner brings up a key element of his epistemology, mentioning that on waking up from sleep we bring with us from out of the cosmos a kind of superlogical logic, a supra-consciousness, whose very essence is a kind of will. This will guides thinking, so that thinking can have an inner order and rightness. Again, normal consciousness proceeds serenely unaware of what supports and sustains it. The will in question is not the hard will by which we undertake bodily efforts and work. It is a subtle will, yet a most powerful one, since it guides every good and true feature of the human mind. This will is the very essence of pure thinking—that is, thinking free of all sense perception—and it is our entry point into true reality.

DORNACH, JULY 8, 1921 GA 205

Let us call to mind today aspects of our nature that have to do with humans as beings who think. This characteristic nature of human beings—that we are beings who think—is misunderstood and misinterpreted by contemporary science in a way that is completely false. People imagine that thoughts are something that we make up ourselves, that we produce them. But the essence of our human nature is only accessible to a more precise observation, for our true nature escapes any coarser forms of observation.

If we do consider the human as a being of thought, it is because in our waking state, from waking up until we go to sleep, we accompany all our experiences with thinking, with the content of our thinking. These experiences of thought seem to arise within us while we are awake and to cease while we sleep. If we have the notion that our thoughts are only present when we are awake, and that then they dissolve at night into a region that cannot be investigated, we will never grow clear about our own nature as beings of thought. A more subtle investigation, not even very advanced in terms of my book *How to Know Higher Worlds*, shows that our thought life is not as simple as we normally imagine it to be. Let us compare the normal life of thought that we all know while awake to another element in our consciousness, more difficult for normal consciousnesss to examine: the element of dreaming.

Normally, when we speak about dreams, we don't consider anything more than a very general characterization of what it is to dream. We compare the state of dreaming with that of wakeful thinking and find that in dreaming there are arbitrary chains of thought; images connect to one another without the kind of connections that we observe in the external world. We compare what happens in a dream with what happens in the outer world, and we see that the former extends beyond the normal range of occurrences.

Certainly people do investigate dreaming up to this point, and even make observations at times with fine results. Yet if we allow ourselves to get familiar with states of absorption, if we let ourselves go a bit and allow our thoughts to roam freely, we can perceive that even in the normal course of thought, related as it is to the course of outer events, there is something involved that is not dissimilar to dreaming, even while we are awake. We can even say that there is a kind of dreaming that takes place all the time between our waking up and our falling asleep—even as we attempt to adapt our thoughts to the outer events around us.

It is as if there were two currents: an upper current that we control as we like, and a lower current that actually passes along just as dreams do in their sequences of images. Of course, you do have to become attentively immersed in the inner life to some degree in order to observe what I am talking about here. Yet it is always present; you can always notice that this undercurrent is there. Thoughts interweave there just as they intermingle in dreams, in the wildest confusion. All kinds of memories may arise, and just as in dreams they can evoke and link up with other thoughts based merely on a similarity of sounds. And people who are too easy on themselves, who don't bother to adapt their thoughts to their outer circumstances, can notice an inner tendency to devote themselves to these waking dreams.

Such waking dreaming is only different from normal dreaming in that the images are less vivid, more like mental pictures. But in regard to the mutual relationships among the images, such waking dreams are no different from so-called real dreams. There are all kinds of people, from those who never notice this undercurrent of dreaming in their awareness, and whose thoughts are completely guided by the thread of external events, all the way to those who immerse themselves in waking dreams and allow their thoughts to tumble and weave every which way. From these dreamier natures, as they are called, up to the drier folk who only allow in whatever corresponds to a sequence of facts, human nature runs the full spectrum. And we have to admit that a preponderance of what has enriched us in art and literature and so on derives from this undercurrent of waking dreams during the day.

This is one side of the issue, and we must take it into account. When we do so, we become aware that we have within us a continual dreaming, but we merely set limits to it through our interaction with the outer world. And we are also aware that it is essentially our will that accommodates to the outer world, and that brings logic and connection to our otherwise unruly inner mass of thoughts. It is the will that brings logic into our thinking. Still, as I have said, this is just one side of the matter.

The other side is this. With a slight development in our capacity for inner observation we can notice that when we wake up we bring with us something from that state we dwelt in between falling asleep and waking. And with a bit of extra attention we come to notice how we actually wake up out of a sea of thoughts every morning. We do not awaken out of something indistinct, out of darkness for instance; but we actually wake up out of a sea of thoughts that seem to have been very, very definite while we slept, though we cannot hold onto them as we pass over into the state of wakefulness.

And if we pursue these observations further, we can notice that these thoughts we bring with us to some degree out of sleep are very similar to the ideas, the inventions, that we have about something we should carry out in the external world. They are very similar to the moral intuitions I have described in my book *Intuitive Thinking as a Spiritual Path*. In the first kind of thinking [waking dreaming], which accompanies our clearer awareness as a kind of undercurrent, we always have the feeling that we can observe our waking dreams as they boil and churn within us. We cannot say the same of this latter phenomenon [the sea of moral thoughts from which we emerge on waking]. For when we return to our body and the use of our body on waking up, we cannot hold fast to the realm we lived and thought in while asleep.

Anyone who becomes clearly conscious of these aspects of human life will no longer consider thoughts as something composed within the human organism. For the thoughts we emerge from on waking cannot be considered as direct products of the organism; they are something we experience while asleep, while the I and the astral body are torn free of our physical body.

Where are we while sleeping? It is the first question that comes up. With our I and our astral body we are outside our physical and life bodies. If we turn an unprejudiced eye on life, we cannot escape the conclusion that while we are asleep and "outside" ourselves, we are *within* what appears to us, when we turn our senses toward the outer world, as the sensory veil of the world, as everything that the sense qualities offer to us. Only consciousness gets extinguished at this point, in normal life. And we feel why consciousness is extinguished when we wake up in the morning out of this state. We feel ourselves to be weak in our bodies, too weak to maintain within them what we experienced while asleep. The I and the astral body, as they dip down into the physical and life body, cannot hold onto what they have experienced. And as they begin to participate in the experiences of the body, what they went through beforehand disappears. As I said, it is only when we have fresh ideas about the external world, or when we have moral intuitions, that we have something like a direct experience of what we lived in between falling asleep and waking up.

When we consider the matter in this way, we get a clear sense of the difference between our inner world and the outer world. Then some light is thrown on the frequent claim that the external world, in the way it appears to us between waking up and falling asleep, is a kind of illusion, a *maya*. For it is in this world, which now shows us its outer face, that we dwell when we are outside ourselves, out-side our body. Then we dip down into the world that otherwise we perceive only through the senses. So we have to say that this world we perceive through the senses has a foundation, and this founda-tion contains its causes, which are beings. In normal consciousness we are too weak to perceive these causes and beings directly.

Unprejudiced observation is enough to reach quite far into the regions described in *How to Know Higher Worlds*. Unprejudiced observation tells us, for instance, the following. To portray normal thought, I can point to the whole extent of what we experience inwardly in thought from waking up to going to sleep, while relying on outer perception or on our physical sensations of pain and pleas-ure, and so forth. We can represent the thoughts experienced in nor-mal consciousness schematically (see diagram, white). Below this, like a waking dream, there lives and weaves what I spoke of at first, a realm that is not subject to the laws of logic (lower red). Yet when, during sleep, we reside in the outer world—as we know in a kind of memory after waking up, it is again a world of thought, but thoughts that take us up into themselves, that are not in us, but out of which we emerge when we awaken (upper red). So in a sense our normal thinking separates two worlds of thought: an inner and an outer thought world; the latter a world of thought that fills the cosmos which receives us into itself when we sleep. We can call it the cos-mic thought world. The former world is also a kind of thought world; in the next few days we will look into it more closely.

With our normal world of thought, then, we find ourselves placed in a kind of general thought world, separated by a kind of boundary, with part of it within us and part outside us. What is in us appears very clearly as a kind of dream. There is always a chaotic tap-estry of thoughts at the base of our souls—something that is not per-vaded by logic. But normal consciousness cannot perceive the other, external world of thought. It is only to a real spiritual perception

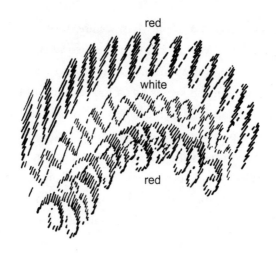

that this outer world of thought can reveal itself as immediate experience. Such perception delves more deeply into the territory described in *How to Know Higher Worlds*. And then we find that the world of thoughts we dive into between falling asleep and waking up is not only as logical as our normal thinking, but even contains a much higher logic. Please do not misunderstand the expression when I say that it is a world of superlogical thoughts. It lies as far above our normal logic as the world of waking dreams lies below logic.

As I have said, this can only be established through spiritual perception. But there is another way in which you can confirm spiritual perception on this point. It must be evident to you that there are regions of one's own organism that normal consciousness cannot reach. As I have recently reported, the fact that we have our normal capacity for memory means that a kind of skin has been drawn over our inner organs. We cannot, through inner observation, investigate our lungs, liver and so forth. . . . So there is something in us that normal consciousness cannot reach. And why not? Because it does not belong exclusively to us. What normal consciousness can reach belongs to us alone. What pulses within our organs belongs not only to us but to us as cosmic beings; it belongs to us and at the same time to all the world.

The following reflection makes this clearer, perhaps. If we look at a person and list the inner organs, the lung and liver and so on, we are dealing with specific forces. They are not merely inner human forces, but universal, cosmic powers. And when everything we know as the outer physical world has disappeared at the conclusion of this Earth, then what now exists as the inner forces of our organs will continue to operate. You could say that everything our eyes see, everything our ears hear, the whole outer world, is a world that will dissolve when the Earth dissolves. What our skin encloses, what we bear within us, contains, spiritually, what will continue when the outer world our senses see is no longer present. Fundamentally, what operates within the human skin is something that outlives the Earth. Within the human skin there lie the centers, the forces, of something that operates outside of earthly existence. We are not only here to enclose our organs for our own sake; we are here as human beings so that the cosmos can form itself within our skin. Our normal consciousness cannot reach it, but we enclose within ourselves something that belongs to the whole world. Is it made up of what we see in the chaotic processes of waking dreams?

We need only consider these chaotic processes of the waking dream to realize that the whole structure of this undercurrent to consciousness is certainly not the architect of our organs, of our organism. The organism would be a sight indeed, if every chaotic component of our subconscious formed our organs and our organism! You would be real caricatures of yourselves, if you were the image of what pulsates through your subconcious. No: just as the outer world, whose superficial aspect we glean through our senses, is built up from the thoughts we experience between falling asleep and waking up, so we ourselves are built from these same forces of thought, inaccessible to normal consciousness.

For a schematic portrayal of the whole of the human being, I would have to draw something like this. There is the surrounding world of thought (see diagram, red). It builds up the human organism, and this human organism gives rise to the world of flowing, higher thought (white). This turns toward the outer sensory *maya* between our own thoughts and the surrounding world (blue).

Try to impress upon yourselves how consciousness embraces only a small part of you, and a greater part of you is built up from the world you enter between falling asleep and waking up. A really unprejudiced view of the human being enables us to see this from still another standpoint, to which I have often alluded.

Normal consciousness gives us access only to our thoughts. Even our feelings are like dreams that swim underneath our thoughts. Feelings ebb and flow. We don't see into them as clearly as we see into our thoughts. But what really resembles our experience of sleep is what we know during the day of our will. What do we know about how we use the will to move a hand or an arm? We know about it only in terms of the mental picture of the action: I want to move my arm. That is a mental picture. We know how it looks when we do move our arm—another mental picture. Normal consciousness is only aware of a sequence of mental images; beneath this there is the flow of feelings. Our will, however, is just as asleep while the rest of us is awake as when we are altogether asleep.

But *what* is asleep? What is asleep down there within us, built into us from the outer cosmos, sleeps in the same way that the minerals and plants are sleeping all around us. That is, we don't penetrate into them from the outside; we can't see into what has cosmic significance for us. From the time we fall asleep to the moment we wake up, we live and weave within this cosmic element. And to the

same degree that we see into the outer world, we can really live within our own organism. To this same degree, then, we cease having mere memories of the events in our lives, and instead we receive inner images of the forces that constitute our organs, lungs, liver, stomach and so on. To the same degree that we come to know the outer world intimately, we also learn to know our own piece of cosmos, which we have incorporated within our own skins—though normal consciousness knows nothing of it.

What is it that we take from the cosmos every morning when we wake up? What we take with us is experienced very clearly by an unprejudiced observer as *will*. And the fundamental distinction between our waking life of thought and what streams beneath it dreamily in the subconscious is that our wakeful thinking is permeated by will. It is the will that brings in logic, and logic is at base not about thoughts, but about how the will orders and unites the images of thought in a certain order, which then corresponds to the course of the cosmos. When we wake up with a dream it is especially easy to see this whirlwind of chaotic, illogical images, and we can perceive directly how a certain kind of will penetrates into the inner chaos. This will orders what is within us in a logical way. We don't carry along with us what I have called cosmic or superlogical logic, we only take with us this will.

Now, how does it come about that this will operates logically within us? This is an important human mystery, something extraordinarily significant. When we dive into the cosmic existence that is not perceptible to ordinary consciousness, when we dive into our organism as a whole, then we feel in our will, which is spread out in this way, the cosmic logic of our organs. It is extraordinarily important to be clear about this. When we wake up every morning, that is, when we dive back down into our bodies, we are forced by this process to bring our will into a certain shape. If our body were not already constituted in a specific shape, then when we awoke our will would be in a tortuous state of chaos. It would do its striving chaotically in all directions. It does not do so because it dives back down into the existing form of the human body. It takes on all these forms, and that gives it a logical structure. This is what makes it possible for the will to give logical order to the thoughts that would otherwise swirl about chaotically. At night, while we are asleep, we are integrated into the superlogic of the cosmos. We cannot hold onto it, however. When we wake up, our will takes the form of the body, just as when you pour water into a pot, and the water takes the form of the pot. But the will flows into every tiniest vein and capillary. . . . It does not only take on the resting form and bump up against the sides of the container; in the human being, this will integrates itself into all the branches of the organism, and from there it controls the course of images, which would otherwise be chaotic.

What we perceive as our inner undercurrent is, in a sense, apart from the body. Of course it is bound up with the body in a sense, but it continually tries to free itself from the body, to come loose from the structures of the body. But what we carry out into the cosmos from our bodies during sleep, and what returns to the body on waking, is something that conforms itself to the law of the body.

Now, if it were only a question of the human head, with its powers of organization, we would only have images. It is a common physiological prejudice to imagine that we reason and make judgments with our heads. No: we only have mental pictures with our heads. If we only had heads, and the whole body were not active in our cognitive process, then we would all be waking dreamers. The head can only engage in waking dreams. And when we enter back into our bodies in the morning, we go by way of our heads—we pass through them, and so bring our dreams with us into consciousness. It is only when we enter more deeply into our bodies, when the will conforms itself not only to our heads but to the rest of our organism, that the will is once again in a position to bring logic into the imagistic forces that would otherwise swirl around within themselves.

This leads to something that I have mentioned in the past. We have to be clear about how we make mental images with our heads, and that we actually make judgments, strange as it may sound, with our legs and hands; we reason with our legs and hands. This is how a judgment, a conclusion is reached. When we make mental pictures, it is just an image reflected in the head; but we reason and make judgments with our whole selves, not only the head. (Of course this does not mean that someone crippled, or missing a limb, has less in the way of reasoning ability). In order to bring what a person is in terms of soul and spirit into connection with the whole of the person, we have to realize how we bring logic into our mental life from the regions normal consciousness cannot reach—regions that are encompassed by our feeling and our will. Reason and judgment occur from out of our inmost realms of sleep, where feeling and willing also have their origins.

The most cosmic region within us is the mathematical. The mathematical region belongs to us not only when we are at rest, but when we move about. We always move in mathematical figures. If we see this in an external way in someone who is walking, then it is something spatial. But if we experience it inwardly, we experience inner mathematics, which are cosmic and which also build us up from within. The spatial relationships we have externally also build us up, and we can experience them within ourselves. And in experiencing them, in abstracting these images that mirror themselves in our brains, we weave them together with whatever reveals itself to us spatially in the world outside.

It is necessary to point out, in our time, that what we posit in the world as mathematical relationships is of a cosmic nature; it is what builds us. A senseless Kantianism has made space into a mere subjective form, but it is not a subjective form; it is something that we experience as real in the same region where we experience the will. From there it shines toward us. Its shining toward the world is something we can then use to penetrate whatever reveals itself to us outwardly.

But in today's world we are far away from understanding how to study this inner interweaving of the human being and the cosmos. I pointed it out in a very obvious way in my *Philosophy of Freedom*, where in certain special passages you can find that beneath everyday consciousness the human being is connected with the whole cosmos. We are an element of the whole cosmos; from out of the universal cosmic realm the individual human blossoms forth, which we then enclose in normal awareness. This is the point that has been understood by the fewest readers; most have been unaware of what I meant. This is no wonder in an age in which abstraction goes to the point of pedantry. It is no wonder in an age where an absolutely abstract view, insightful as it may be in many ways, is presented to the world as something special, that what leads into reality, into true reality, is not understood.

Ideas such as those given here are an invitation to a kind of thinking that meets reality in an adequate way. They may be ridiculed by those who are trained to think abstractly. For the last three or four centuries, Western humanity has been trained in mere abstraction. But in our age, a turning point has to come about, so that we find our way back to reality. People have become materialistic, and not because they have lost logic, but because they have lost reality. Materialism is logical; spiritualism is logical; monism is logical; dualism is logical; everything is logical if it contains no outright errors of thought. But its being logical doesn't make it correspond to reality. Reality can only be found if we take our thinking more and more into the region I have described by saying, "In pure thinking we hold the universal world process by one corner." That is what I say in my epistemological works, and it has to be achieved as the basis of an understanding of the world.

The moment when you are still thinking, even though you have no sensory content in view, is the moment when thinking becomes will. There is no difference any more between thinking and willing. For thinking is a kind of willing, and willing is a kind of thinking. When thinking has become completely free of sensory elements, then you have caught hold of the universal world process by one corner. And this is what we have to strive toward above everything else: to arrive at the concept of pure thinking.

CHAPTER SEVEN

Preparing for a New Birth

〰〰〰

WE PASS ABOUT *a third of our life asleep, or eight hours out of every twenty-four. This familiar fact is rarely the subject of adequate astonishment. All over the world, people of all kinds lie down on those flat places and disappear from normal activity for hours at a time. What is going on? Why do we need it? What are we up to during all that sleep? The challenge of Steiner's view is that we are not inactive at night, but supremely active.*

Instead of the subjective, selfish coloration by which we view our lives during the day, nighttime consciousness is both more universal and more moral. Our prime activity during the night is self-review. We carefully scroll backward through the previous day, finding and savoring each moment of significance (and what moment has none?). According to Steiner, we do this through the grace of higher beings who accompany and guide this process.

The period called "death"—the period between two incarnations— involves us in a similar backward-scrolling review. Again in the company of higher beings, we review our lifetime of sleep. This review is a preparation for later stages of "death" where we turn aside from our biography and immerse ourselves still less selfishly in the spiritual beings and mean-ings around us.

The cumulative effect of Steiner's teaching here is to turn human existence inside out, like looking at the back of a carpet. What was for-merly the figure becomes the background, and what was previously the background emerges into new prominence. Earthly life is an interlude between spiritual states—sleep and death—that permeate and surround it. "Our little life is rounded with a sleep." And yet instead of diminish-ing this little life, the spiritual context makes us marvel at the chance we have on Earth, and give thanks for the opportunity to love.

———•———

STUTTGART, JUNE 21,1923 GA 224

If we consider human existence on Earth, the most significant ele-ment in life must appear to be our capacity to think or make mental images—the capacity to think for ourselves about the world, our own actions and so forth. Any other view would be a self-deception. Certainly there are temptations to consider other aspects of life as more valuable. We can feel, just below the threshold of conscious-ness, that our feelings about our own tasks, about our relationships and about the world, are more valuable than our thinking. And if we consider our moral existence, and the voice of conscience, we can tell ourselves that this conscience speaks to us from depths that thinking can never reach.

We may feel all the more inclined to such a view when we see that even the most highly trained thinking, schooled in accordance with normal life, cannot arrive at the moral impulses of a simple, unschooled conscience. Still, we would be fooling ourselves if we imagined that thoughts are not the essence of human life on Earth.

Certainly the voice of conscience, the feeling of compassion, come from inexpressibly deeper sources than our thoughts. Yet these impulses that well up from the depths only find their right place in the human sphere when they are permeated by thought. The voice of conscience, too, only finds its true value by living within our thoughts, so that we clothe in thoughts what the voice of conscience says. Without overestimating thought, we still have to acknowledge, if we want to proceed in describing human consciousness without illusion, that it is thinking that makes us human. So Hegel is right, in a sense, when he says that thinking distinguishes man from beast.

Let us consider the total compass of the thoughts that fill us from the moment we wake to the point of going to sleep. If we are honest about it, we will have to say that the majority of our thoughts in life are dependent on what comes from outside, on sense impressions and experiences that have to do with the material processes of earthly life. Our thoughts pass by in intimate connection with the Earth, so that whatever is most significant for us between birth and death seems to be connected to the Earth. But if we consider the totality of human life on Earth, we notice that a third of it goes by without any thoughts at all. If, with the means available to ordinary consciousness, we look back over a period of life, we naturally link one day's experience to the next and leave out the experiences of sleep that remain in the unconscious. But this leaves a third of life out of consideration.

From my earlier lectures you know that our activity during sleep, though unconscious, is not uneventful. The I and the astral body go through experiences at night that simply do not light up within our awareness. And if we look more closely, we notice that the unconscious forces that operate during sleep continue while we are awake—though we might say they live a life of sleep, for they operate in our whole activity of will, which is no clearer to us than the state of sleep. And they operate in a large portion of our feeling life, which is a kind of dreaming.

When we try to look at what comes from our deepest essence, from our fundamental nature, we have to look at something uncon-scious. Through spiritual scientific observation, we find that what operates in us while we sleep continues to operate while we are awake. It is present as the I and the astral body, though they do not enter ordinary awareness except in their effects—the expressions of our will and our feeling life—which give a special aspect to what does enter into clear, waking awareness: our life of thought. This becomes more comprehensible when we take into consideration the existence we participate in between death and rebirth.

When we pass through the gates of death, we undergo states I have described to you before, and that you already know in some of their aspects. If we examine very precisely what element of the human being is necessary for our thinking, our conceptual life, we arrive at the insight that for the formation of thoughts on Earth we need the physical body. The physical body must be set in action for us, as earthly human beings, to have thoughts. Beyond this, we also need to set our life body in action. But these are the two elements of human nature that seem to lie unconscious in bed while we sleep. Only when our consciousness has developed somewhat, through a certain training of our soul, and when we can even see physical things from a spiritual viewpoint, do we realize that actually we are thinking all the time, even when we are asleep. If we consider the *whole* human being, we can say that during earthly life we are never not thinking.

When we return in the morning to our physical and life bodies, normal consciousness forces itself very quickly back into them, and it is only then that normal consciousness becomes aware of external things—of sense perceptions that we then process conceptually, of objects that we perceive around us. But when we begin to enter much more consciously into our physical and life bodies, then as we awaken we meet the thinking that has gone on while we were asleep. We think; that is, the physical and life bodies are caught up in continual thought activity while we are asleep, only we are not present to it; we are outside this activity in our I and astral body, so we are not aware that it is going on. But this is a great self-deception. And just as we can better recognize any aspect of ourselves when it is torn away from its harmonious relationship to the whole of life— that is, when it appears in an abnormal state—so too we can realize based on external experiences of the world that while we are asleep we not only continue to think, but we think far more cleverly while asleep and absent than when awake and present. We arrive at the depressing fact that our life body thinks less well when we are within it, with the normal consciousness of our I and astral body. We spoil the thoughts that course through our life body by being present to them with our normal consciousness.

Someone who can see into these things can therefore confirm reports like the following. There were once two university students. One was a philologist and knew nothing of numbers. The other was a mathematics student. Now, we know that at certain moments in the study of mathematics, you do sweat through certain problems, wheareas in philology it tends to go more easily. And that's how it was with these two students, who shared a room. One night, at the end of their preparations for their exams, the philology student was very pleased with himself, while the mathematics student was not, since he couldn't solve a problem he needed to solve for a written assignment. So he lay down to sleep very dissatisfied, and a strange event followed. At a certain hour the philology student woke up and saw the mathematics student get out of bed and walk to the desk. There, he thought some more, wrote for a long time and then went back to bed and slept. The next day, when they both got up, the mathematics student said, "We didn't drink anything last night, but this morning I have a terrible headache." The other replied, "No wonder, if you get up at three and do calculations for hours, of course your head will swim the next day." And his roommate said, "I was not up in the night!" He knew nothing about having been up. Then he looked and saw that he had solved the problem, though he had no memory of it.

These things are not fairy tales. I chose this example, which belongs to the literature, because you can check it. I could tell you many other such things. It is not a question of the individual example, but of the reality of all this. When consciousness is not present—and I emphasize that the person in question had no memory of his nocturnal activity—then the physical and life bodies are worked on by outside influences, and the life body works in the physical body to solve the assigment.

Now, I know that many will wish this kind of thing could happen more often. But we today do not have it so easy. In such a case as this the life body proves to be much more clever when it is left alone to work on the physical body than when the I and the astral body are present. This was merely an illustration of how we go on thinking all through the night. For our thoughts are stimulated directly by the outer world through the mediation of the life body, and then the physical body helps as well, to raise up thoughts for the physical human being on Earth.

So our thought life is definitely bound up with our physical and life bodies. Not so our feeling life and our will life. It is merely a superstition of modern science to imagine that our feeling and will are as bound up with our physical and life bodies as our thoughts are. I will only review a few points on this topic.

In contemporary earthly life, it is not true to say we can survey what happens with our I and our astral body when they separate from the physical and life bodies, taking with them from normal life only the will and a portion of the life of feeling. For this experience between going to sleep and waking up takes place in a completely different world. It takes place in a spiritual world, a world in which the environment is not the kingdoms of nature, the mineral kingdom and the plant kingdom, but the higher hierarchies, spiritual beings, spiritual events. But as long as we are beings of the Earth, we are not adequately developed to survey what we are experiencing in our I and astral body between falling asleep and waking up. The experience stays unconscious, but it is not less lively than what becomes conscious. We do go through it. And once we have done so, it is something that belongs to our inner content. Each morning we awaken changed; the night has changed us. We don't awaken in the same state we arrived at before going to sleep. Instead, we awaken in the state that our sleep life has put us into.

Now, when we pass through the gates of death, we lay down our physical and life bodies. And so, in the first days after death (since it takes about three days to let go of the life body), we feel that our thought life is being sucked up by the universe. First, we have a brief glance over our previous earthly life. It is as if our past life were the world around us; we see it in pictures before us. The whole of the past life stands before us at one stroke once the soul is free of the physical and life bodies, that is, once our passage through the gate of death has been accomplished. But it still takes days afterward for the life body to be completely dissolved in the general life processes of the universe.

During this time, our impression is, first, of a living and sharply contoured overview of the life. Then it grows weaker and weaker, but at the same time more "cosmic," until after a few days it finally melts away. But in these few days, the most valuable aspect of the earthly life that is past departs from the person who has died. Everything we thought about the things of the world, about our whole earthly environment, what filled our normal consciousness—all this melts away from us in just a few days. And to the exact extent that the content of earthly life melts away, there emerges the content of what we all go through unconsciously every night during sleep. This content now begins to become conscious for us. If we really experienced nothing during our sleep life, then three or four days after death our conscious life would be at an end. For everything we thought of as most valuable during our life has melted away, and out of this darkening, dimming awareness there emerges what we lived through every time we slept, but which formerly remained outside awareness.

Now, the peculiar characteristic of our sleeping experiences is this: that in sleep the world takes place in reverse. Whether our sleep is long or short, once we fall asleep it is all the same, since other states of consciousness also have completely different time-senses. So the characteristic I am talking about holds true whether you sleep all night or only for a few minutes. From the time we go to sleep until the time we wake up again, we leave backwards through everything we just experienced between our last waking and the current moment of falling asleep. But we live through it in a different form than we did at first. When we are awake, we live through the day from start to finish, every event and every circumstance, in terms of physical, intellectual nuances. While asleep, however, we experience it all backwards and in terms of its moral nuances. Moral and religious impulses appear; we pass through everything evaluating how it has made us more or less valuable as moral human beings. We indulge in no illusions, nor can we, but we evaluate everything we did the previous day in terms of our fundamental humanity.

Natural science is wrong when it claims that human life relies on causality, on necessary consequences, though in waking life we may only see this linking of cause and effect. Reality contains another current, though it remains unconscious for us during the day, and every night as we sleep we experience this moral ordering of the world. There, we evaluate things morally, that is, in connection with our own human value. We do this every night, or every time we sleep, with regard to the last-experienced period of being awake. And when we pass through the gates of death, then we go backwards through the last night, the next-to-last night, the night before that, and so on, up to the first night after we were born when we became conscious for the first time—for about a third of the time we were alive, since we slept through about a third of our earthly life.

The physical, cause-and-effect course of the world passes away from us, and what rises up before us is the course of the world as the gods and spirits think about it, feel about it and will it. Still, it appears to us bearing the coloration that earthly life gave it, since we have to pass through it in the form in which we lived it during our life on Earth. We need about a third of our lifetime to live it over again backwards in this way, just as I described it in my book *Theosophy*. There, I described the land of the soul and the world of the soul.

For before we enter a world that is completely spiritual, we have to live through everything that we experienced on Earth unconsciously in our sleeping state. In this way, we are training our awareness for the actual spiritual experiences between death and rebirth. At the same time, this backward experience of earthly life frees us from earthly life. Until we have done this, our consciousness is not adequately free to move among the spirits of the higher worlds. And once we have come to this point, we are only at the beginning of our life in the higher worlds.

Our life in the higher worlds, until we come to Earth again, can become a purely spiritual experience. Just as here we live among physical beings and events, there we live in a spiritual world among spiritual beings and spiritual events. We live among the spiritual beings and deeds that never descend to Earth, and among the spiritual beings who as human beings came to Earth and passed through the gates of death before us, or even after us. We meet again with all the people we knew during earthly life. And this community of ours is very widespread. For through our sleep life we include in this community everything that we only touched on briefly with human beings during our life on Earth. In sleep, we already live within the spiritual world, but we are still experiencing earthly events in reverse as earthly human beings; just this distinguishes our nightly experience from what we go through once we have passed through the gates of death.

First, we have to acknowledge that in the first few days, the content of our earthly consciousness melts away from us. The unconscious experiences of sleep, which we ignored during life, now emerge and we really do experience them. For in those earthly states of sleep, we experience backwards, and in pictures, only the events of waking life. As we step through the gates of death, we submerge ourselves in spiritual substance, just as here we submerge ourselves in material substance. Just as we have the physical and life bodies on Earth, after death we receive a higher kind of external sheath, a spiritual sheath. Through this process, we can actually go through, in a real way, what we only pass through in pictures, in images, during our periods of sleep on Earth. It is a real, true experience, just as real as our experience of earthly life in a physical body. This real experience, a repetition in reality of the pictorial experience of our sleep states, is the basis of the further experiences we go through in the later course of our life between death and rebirth.

What follows between death and rebirth, after we have put aside our whole earthly existence, is a preparation for the next life on Earth. In conjunction with the beings of the spiritual world, we form the spiritual seed of our next earthly life, and above all our next physical body. Then comes another period in which we grow oriented toward life on Earth. After dwelling for a long time among spiritual beings and spiritual facts, something happens that can be compared to a feeling of tiredness, of wanting to go to sleep. We feel how the awareness we have in the spirit becomes weaker, how we can no longer work together with the beings of the spiritual world in the way we have done, and our consciousness shifts over to an interest in a new life on Earth.

Just as every day we sink into the unconsciousness of sleep, our purely spiritual consciousness that fills most of our time between death and rebirth sinks down, not to unconsciousness but toward being filled with interest for life on Earth—as seen from the other side, from the point of view of the spiritual world. This interest in earthly life emerges many years, even many centuries, before we descend again to an actual life on Earth. The interest we took for so long in the purely spiritual world transforms itself into an interest in the succession of generations, and at the end of this succession, we ourselves are to be born. From out of the spiritual world, we take note of our ancestors through many long years before our own parents are born. So from out of the spiritual world we grow together with our ancestry.

At some point all this will become common knowledge, and only then will we see how limited today's science really is, despite its partial correctness, with regard to the concept of inheritance. Physical inheritance can only become comprehensible to us when we understand the role of those forces by which we participated in our ancestry from out of the spiritual world. When we point out here, with our limited scientific means, that we possess this or that characteristic of our great-grandfather's, we shouldn't forget that while this great grandfather was alive, we took an interest in him from out of the spiritual world; we grew together with what played itself out as the characteristics of the succeeding generations. We grew into it from out of the spiritual world.

When anthroposophy makes itself felt in the general civilization of humanity, these things will gain practical significance. We hardly realize how much in the way of cowardice and lack of energy derives today unconsciously from our notions of inheritance, for our science can only speak of inherited characteristics in a completely inadequate way. It has even permeated our arts, the whole of human thought.

When we finally penetrate to a realization of how we have been connected to the physical formation of our own ancestors, and also to the development of our own soul, which from out of the spiritual world has followed and co-created the whole evolution of our ancestors, then this awareness will become an inward reality for us. Then energy and courage will come from the spirit into our souls, where today we derive only cowardice and lack of energy from our contemporary style of thought. For it is not of the slightest value if we think this or that theoretically about the spiritual world. For the most part, we even clothe whatever we think about the spiritual world in physical thought forms. It is not a question of our making theoretical thoughts for ourselves about the spiritual world. . . . What matters is not that we have mere thoughts about the spiritual world—we have to have them initially, so that the content of the spiritual world enters our souls at all—but that these thoughts become living and creative forces within us. Normal physical thoughts on Earth are completely abstract. Most scientific thoughts are abstract; they accomplish nothing within our human nature—no more than mirror images. Such thoughts are only pictures. If you are standing with another person, looking in a mirror, and the other person smacks you on the ear, you won't ascribe the blow to what happens in the mirror, but to the real person standing next to you. Thoughts are like these mirror images: they don't *do* anything, they don't act as impulses on reality. It is moral intuitions that can act as impulses. So, even if we have to start from thoughts, our thoughts about the spiritual world have to be active, active as reality itself and not like other thoughts.

We only enter into the real anthroposophic view when we sense and experience thoughts as realities. A common objection arises at this point. It can be stated superficially that the whole anthroposophical world view is based on auto-hypnosis, a kind of self-suggestion. People say for instance that some of us are so suggestive that the very thought of drinking lemonade can fill us with the feeling of drinking a real lemonade. It is true that there are people so sensitive that they can taste lemonade in their mouths when they think about lemonade. This seems to be a good objection, but just let someone tell us about quenching thirst by the mere thought of lemonade! Mere thoughts do not become realities. As long as anthroposophy remains mere thought, it is like an imaginary lemonade. But it need not remain so, for it derives from spiritual reality. It does not simply operate like a thought, but it operates the way outer reality operates on material substances. It permeates, it resonates through our human life of feeling and of will. It becomes a reality in us. This is what matters.

So we don't have much if we have anthroposophy as theory. It has to become life. It is life if it fills our souls with energy, perseverance, courage. It is life if, faced with the cares of physical life on Earth—in our deepest sorrow, our deepest suffering—we become filled with inner joy, inner consolation, inner energy by looking up toward the spiritual world. Then anthroposophy becomes like a living being; it becomes something that seems to move amongst us as a living being. Only then has it become amongst us what it should be, permeating all our activity. And then it helps us to permeate this world in which we have come for the sake of the spirit, not for the sake of physical matter. Above all, anthroposophy arrives at real knowledge of what we are as human beings.

CHAPTER EIGHT

Dreaming and the Etheric Body

FAMILIAR THEORIES OF dream suggest that in dreaming we recall our experiences of the past day. Steiner puts forward the view that dreams are potentially the review of our whole lives, since everything we have experienced is contained in the life body, to which our attention turns during part of the time we are asleep. This life body contains a living record of all we have experienced during our lives on Earth to date.

To convey the inner activity necessary to understand what lies behind our dreams, Steiner uses a somewhat confusing but typical image. He says it is as if we were to write a letter, but did not understand the words of the letter until we had finished writing. This is very unlike our normal process of first understanding what we have to say, then writing it down. The reason for the reversal in dream life or spiritual perception is that it is not we ourselves who are writing. Instead, through our intensive inner activity, we actually begin to participate in the presence of the beings who are writing our dreams within us.

This ability to perceive our dreams actively, and so to understand what stands behind them, Steiner relates to the ability we need if we are to maintain any self-awareness after death. To see our way in the night is to see our way through death. We need only one tool for this job, but it is the hardest to acquire: we need a strengthened attentiveness, a power of thinking that far exceeds normal awareness. Steiner pointed in the same direction in his epistemological works, such as Intuitive Thinking as a Spiritual Path. We should recall that he wanted this book, in English translation, to bear the title The Philosophy of Spiritual Activity, so as to underline the active receptivity required for the mind to reach its own sources. Compared with all other spiritual currents of our time, Steiner's writings may place the greatest emphasis on strength, on energetic acquisition of mental power. But this is not a macho power: it is the power of a strengthened receptivity.

Just as he initially points to a perception of the etheric or life body, Steiner later shows how we perceive elements of our astral or starry body in sleep. We see our own incompleteness, the way in which this member of the human organism reflects our moral and spiritual shortcomings. We may also solve problems and come to mathematical insights through an intensified dream life, for the astral body contains, as Steiner says, all of mathematics—not only the mathematics that is already known, but the mathematics yet to be discovered.

Again and again, Steiner emphasizes the role of active, conscious, transparently clear thinking as the basis for spiritual perception and growth. The same direction, the same fundamental meditative style, unlocks the secrets of dreams as it unlocks the secrets of the physical and all other worlds. It is the path of active thinking that begins at the level of everyday thinking but intensifies it limitlessly. Through such practice (he points particularly to Intuitive Thinking as a Spiritual Path and to The Threshold of the Spiritual World as texts that help us on the way), we arrive not at greater mysteries but at greater clarities. We become united with what formerly seemed other and separate from us. We lose ourselves in absorption, but through that very process find ourselves far more securely rooted and grounded than the "self" of everyday life.

BERLIN, APRIL 18, 1914 GA 154

If you remember a dream clearly, you will notice that as the dream flowed on, you were a kind of observer of the images weaving past your soul—yet without there being any definite "I" to observe them. In dreams, the sense of "I" does not emerge as markedly as in waking consciousness.

The dream tapestry of moving images presents the soul with two kinds of scenes. On the one hand, there are scenes that are well known to the dreamer, since they relate to experiences of recent days, sometimes transforming these in the most varied ways, even to the point of unrecognizability. On the other hand, there are dreams that present us with something altogether new and different from our past experiences. Still, in every case we have the sense that living, weaving images revealed themselves as they passed by our soul. We recall these images upon waking. Some we hold longer in memory; some are extinguished by the events of the day.

Today we want to pose and answer an unusual question: *Where do we perceive our dreams?* When we're awake in the physical world, we know that, whatever we perceive, we are perceiving it in the world we call physical. But what is the "substance," so to speak, in which we dream? What corresponds there to the things and processes of the physical world when we are awake?

It is what we call the "etheric" world, the ether that permeates the entire world with its inwardness, and everything that lives within it. This is the substance within which we perceive when we are dreaming. But as a rule, we only perceive a particular part of the etheric in our dreams. The etheric world is closed off from us in waking consciousness, when we are perceiving things physically; that is, we don't perceive the ether through our physical senses, though it is all around us. In the same way, the ether all around us remains imperceptible to normal dreaming. Only the part of the etheric world that is our own etheric body appears to us when we dream.

When we sleep, after all, we are outside our physical and etheric bodies. And the normal dream consists in our looking back, from what is now outside our physical and etheric bodies, onto what we have left behind in sleep. But looking at ourselves in this way, we do not notice the physical body—we are, after all, not using our physical senses. Instead, neglecting our physical body, we look back and see only our etheric body. What appear to us as dreams are, at base, the processes in the etheric body that have lifted their veil at this or that spot. Most dreams are really like this: in sleep, one beholds one's own etheric body, and some part of its incredibly complex processes comes to awareness and makes up a dream.

This etheric body of ours is something extraordinarily complicated. Within it, for example, all our memories are kept continually present. Even what has sunk deep within us into the depths of the soul, and would never normally emerge into daytime consciousness, is somehow contained there. The whole of our life in the present incarnation is contained in the etheric body. Admittedly, it is hard to imagine this, but it is still true. Imagine that you were to talk all day long (some people do just this), and everything you say is recorded onto a record. When one record is full, you start on a second, then a third, and so on. You need more records, or fewer ones, depending on how much you speak. We assume now that someone collects all the records, with all of them nicely arranged. Everything you had said during the day could be put on the phonograph in the evening. If someone played them, it would all be played back. In the same way, everything that makes up our memories is simultaneously, continuously present in our etheric body. And let us suppose that, through the special circumstances of sleep (to keep the analogy going), a part of the contents of the etheric body came before our soul as if some part of the records were played on the phonograph.

This would be the dream, the most common kind of dream: our awareness weaving within our own etheric body.

Something similar could be said about many hallucinations. Most of these come about when a person, still dwelling with the I and astral body within the physical body, can nevertheless see a kind of detached portion of the etheric body. It happens in the following way. Imagine that something in your physical body is sick, for example something in your nervous system. Then the etheric body cannot take hold at the point of the nervous system that is sick; it is as if it were expelled from that spot. The etheric body itself is not sick, but it is detached from the physical body at a specific spot. If it were connected to the physical, everything would proceed as in normal consciousness; we would not even guess that the physical body is sick. When the etheric body cannot take hold at a given spot, and what is present there shines out toward the etheric, what emerges into consciousness is a hallucination.

The etheric substance, from which dreams and hallucinations arise, surrounds us everywhere in the world. And our own etheric body is like a piece cut out of the etheric substance surrounding us. When we pass through the gate of death, and lay aside the physical body, then we make our way through this etheric substance. We basically never leave this etheric substance in the whole course of our path from death to a new birth. For this etheric substance is everywhere, and we have to move through it; we are in it. Sometime after death we lay aside our own etheric body, and it dissolves into this same etheric substance. In normal life, we do not possess the capacity to perceive within the outer etheric substance, and in fact we perceive nothing of it. Through dreaming, we make the acquaintance of a self-oriented perception of the etheric.

Real perception within the surrounding etheric world depends on something quite specific. If a person is to really perceive, after death, within the surrounding etheric world, or intentionally develops on Earth so as to receive imaginations clairvoyantly (which means perceiving in the etheric world), then it requires a much greater strength than we normally possess between birth and death, a stronger inner force of the soul. We don't perceive within the etheric world that surrounds us because the force of our soul is too weak. To perceive there at all, we have to make ourselves much more active than is necessary for normal life. After death, too, our soul must be much more active than in normal life if we are to have any environment about us. Otherwise, though the ether is all around us, we don't perceive it. It would be as if in everyday life we had no sense perception. Thus, a person has to possess a more active and forceful soul to manage in the life after death, so as not to be blind and deaf in that world.

We can use a comparison to help us picture how the soul perceives after death or after it has acquired the capacity for imagination. We can use the analogy of writing. When you write something down, there is meaning behind what you have written. You made the signs to signify it, and you can also make it true; you can make what you wrote correspond to something in the objective world. If you want to communicate something to a friend by letter, and write it out so that your friend can read it, then you first have to put down the signs; later, your far-off friend can decipher them and so understand you. If someone came and said, "No, it can't be so! What's written there corresponds to nothing objective in the world. It is simply something written down with no relation to the real world"—that would, of course, be nonsense. Just as you designate an objective fact when you write by first putting down the signs for it, so it is for imaginative thinking in the imaginative world. You have to be active. You first have to set down your signs for the objective processes of the spiritual world, and you have to be aware that you are setting them down. Your doing so depends on your having the necessary strength to live within spiritual reality, so that it stimulates you to write down what is true rather than what is false. But the fact is, you know it is you who are writing it down.

I want to characterize this in still another way. Let us return to the dream. When we dream in normal life, we have the sense that the dream images "weave," that they play themselves out. Recall how you see such dreams: as if the dream images are wafting past your soul. Now imagine you had a different picture of them: that you yourself are putting the dream images in space and time, just as you put down letters on paper. We don't have this impression in normal dreaming or hallucination. You need to have the awareness that you yourself are the governing power in your dreams. You set down the first thing, then add it to the next, just as you write something down on paper. You are the governing power; you make it yourself. Only the power that is behind you (as in writing) can make what you write true.

We have to be clear that the great difference between dreaming, hallucinating and real clairvoyance consists of this: With real clairvoyance, you are continually aware of being yourself the occult writer. What you see is an occult script. You write, into the world, what the world expresses or reveals to you. Naturally, you could object here, "Then you don't have to write it, if you already know it. Why write it down?" But it doesn't work that way. For it is not actually you who writes, but the being of the next-higher hierarchy. You devote yourself to the being of the next-higher hierarchy, and that is the power that holds sway. In a completely inward process of the soul, you write down what rules within you in this way. And by then contemplating what has been written in the occult script, what was to be expressed is revealed to you.

I have often emphasized in public lectures that the development of clairvoyance, in fact all perception, is something active. It cannot stay at the level of passive absorption adequate to cognition in the physical world. In this way you gradually come to know what we spoke of at the beginning of our anthroposophical life together, that is, "learning the occult script"—which I wrote down later in a more exact form in *The Threshold of the Spiritual World*. The force of soul necessary to write the occult script into spiritual space and spiritual time is a stronger, more powerful force of soul; it must be stronger, more powerful than the force of soul we apply to perception in normal life. And we have to have this force once we have gone through the gates of death. Whoever wants to acquire imaginative clairvoyance develops this force through meditation and gradually attains it. In this way, we arrive at what has just been described; we experience a world of which one weak reflection is the dream.

Yet we arrive there in such a way that we are in control in our dreams, just as we are in control when we make a table or a shoe, where we put the pieces together. If so many people complain, "I've tried all possible meditation but I'm not becoming clairvoyant," it is simply because they don't want what I have just been describing. They are happy not to have any need for it. They don't want to develop inwardly active soul forces, but want to become clairvoyant without having to acquire a stronger force of soul. They want the tableau that is to arise through their clairvoyance to come up all by itself. But then it would be nothing more than a hallucination or a dream. A dream is a piece of the etheric world that you can take from one place, grasp with your etheric antennae and set down in another place. It doesn't belong in real clairvoyance at all.

In the experience of real clairvoyance, you feel *inside* it, in the same way you feel when you write on paper in the physical world. The difference is this: When you want to write on paper in the physical world, you must first know what you want to write (or at least, it is generally good to know in advance), while in spiritual perception you allow the beings of the hierarchies to write. What you are to perceive only appears to you as you begin to write it down. No real clairvoyance can come about unless you yourself actively participate in every atom of what you behold. You must be actively present yourself.

And we need this kind of power—the ability to write in the etheric—when we pass through the gates of death. All the thinking that we exercise in the normal physical world, and that serves us there, is of no use for perception after death. Someone may be clever, thoughtful and quick-witted about things in the physical world, but the power of this kind of thinking is much too weak to be able to write with it in the etheric world. All the notions we develop here and relate to physical things come from the kind of weak thinking power that is of no use after death. We have to have a stronger power of thought that activates itself within us—a power of thought, in other words, that can make thoughts that represent nothing whatsoever from the outer, sensory world. If we didn't have something within us that allows us to make thoughts unrelated to what is external—thoughts that instead rise up within as if from the depths of our soul—if we couldn't make such thoughts for ourselves, then our capacities after death would be inadequate.

You might say, "All right. Then you could think up anything, any fantasy. You could strain your powers of fantasy and cook up all kinds of thoughts that represent no external thing. That would be a good preparation for the requisite thought power after death." Or you might say, "I want to have a lot of thought power after death. So I'll imagine a winged dragon that doesn't exist, terrifying beasts, and so forth. I'll imagine it all, since I don't want to be tied to the apron strings of external representation; I'll imagine the wildest things. I'll develop the inner power of thinking and prepare myself for a strengthened thinking after death." I won't deny that if you did all this, you would have more capacities in the world after death than someone who did nothing. But you would only perceive illusions, errors, like someone with a diseased eye who has to perceive the physical world falsely, or like someone with a diseased ear who has to perceive the tones of the physical world incorrectly. Someone who exercised this kind of fantasy would condemn himself or herself to perceive the most grotesque nonsense in the etheric world, but not what really has its roots in the etheric.

In earlier eras of human development, care was always taken that people should have conceptions that are not borrowed from the physical world but are also not concocted from arbitrary fantasy. The great founders of religions who have appeared in the course of our development were always careful to provide such images to humanity. By transmitting such concepts, related not to the physical but to supersensible worlds, they enabled those who followed them to develop ideas independent of the sense world that were nonetheless true, since they had been drawn from the supersensible world. That is the greatness, the power of human pedagogy through these founders of religion. To characterize them properly we could say that they had the task of transmitting to humans concepts of just such a kind so that they would not arrive blind and deaf in the spiritual world after death. So we can see that their concern was for human beings to be completely alive, completely conscious, not to have an awareness that must grow dim, err or even extinguish itself after the hour of death.

But today, as I have often put it, we live in a cycle of human development in which humans have come of age. No longer will founders of religions appear in the old style and appeal to human faith. That belonged to ages past—though such ages extend into our own time, of course. Currently, the experience of the new life can only begin with a smaller number of people, since many will find this difficult, and even long for the old traditions.

We live in the time when human beings should come of age. The more recent spiritual science will offer something to replace what the founders of religions transmitted through belief. To prevent misunderstanding, let us emphasize that Christ is an exception from among these "founders of religion." For, as I have often pointed out, with Christ it is not a question of what he taught but of what happened through him. The old founders of religion were generally teachers; Christ set his own power inside human beings through the Mystery of Golgotha. But today this is very hard for many people to grasp. That is why they speak of Christ merely as a great world teacher, which is simply nonsense for someone who really understands the whole meaning of the Christ.

Human beings are coming of age. It will happen through spiritual science, through concepts, ideas and understandings that relate to our life after death and so to the whole life of the soul. Spiritual science can be achieved by every human being, as long as he or she truly develops in the sense of spiritual science. It strives to give only what each soul can attain for itself—not, as earlier, by listening to the great founders. And even if, today, there are only a few researchers who can produce and communicate spiritual scientific results, these results can then be understood by anyone with the will to do so. There is nothing here you "have to believe." People only say that spiritual science "has to" be believed because they are too full of materialistic prejudices to enter into what spiritual science can really give them. Once you do enter in, you can understand everything and find it comprehensible. You don't need to be clairvoyant; ordinary understanding is also adequate for us gradually to understand everything —of course, this "gradually" will be inconvenient for some.

Unlike the ancient religions, spiritual science appeals to the faculty of human understanding. The teachings of the great founders of religion gave the human soul something that woke it up spiritually, so as to be able to perceive in the etheric world and therefore also to lead a self-aware life after death. And once again, through the more recent spiritual science, the human soul will be able to acquire the power of developing the necessary force of thought after death to perceive the etheric world consciously as its environment. The human being of today who has the will to understand spiritual science, like the human being of yesterday who listened to the founder of a religion, is armed with the capacity to know his or her way around properly after death. There is only *one* kind of human being who will find it hard to be oriented after death; for this kind of person, life after death will be largely clouded and darkened. I am speaking of the confirmed materialist, who wants only to cling to the things and images of the normal physical world, who does not want to acquire the power of perceiving in that world we enter after death. In terms of the spirit and soul, to be a materialist is like destroying one's eyes and ears—killing off one's own senses—and yet continuing to live. It is as if one were to say, "These eyes are worthless; they only give impressions of light—away with them! These ears are only good for perceiving fluctuations in the air, not the truth—away with them! Away with the senses, one after the other!" Once you go to the sources of spiritual-scientific understanding, this is not difficult to realize.

Today I have tried to characterize for you, from a particular standpoint, what it is like to stand within the spiritual world. I would like now to add another point. From the world of dreams we can isolate one kind that everyone knows from experience: this is the kind of dream in which, to some extent, we meet ourselves. Normal dreams flow past, as I have described them, with the dream weaving its way before us while we have no clear awareness of self; only later do we think back over the course of the dream with any awareness of "I." You can test this for yourself. But there are also dreams in which we face ourselves objectively, so to speak. It is not only that we see ourselves, but something else as well. For example, one may dream of a student who sits in school, unable to solve a problem in arithmetic. Then someone else comes by and solves it easily. This is the dream, but you can see that it is the student who actually comes in and solves the problem. So as dreamers we confront ourselves, but we do not recognize ourselves (which is not the essential point here). In such a case, it is as if the human "I" splits in two. It would be nice if the same thing happened in the physical world. Then, when you didn't know something, the other "I" could come and tell you perfectly easily. In dreams, it can happen. This kind of dream has its own special character.

In dreams, as we know, we are outside our physical and etheric body, in our astral body and "I." In the dreams we discussed earlier, it is our own etheric body that floats toward us; the dreams in which we confront ourselves, on the other hand, depend on a piece of the astral body (which we have taken with us) revealing itself to us. So it is a piece of self-perception outside the physical body. While it can certainly happen during sleep that you perceive a piece of your astral body, we normally do not experience our astral body, and there are many things in the astral body that are not conscious for us in normal waking awareness. I have often commented on all that the etheric body includes; it includes everything we have experienced. The astral body, however, even contains what we have *not* experienced. For the astral body is quite a complex formation. It is organized to some extent from out of the spiritual worlds, and contains not only those things that we already have in us now, but also those that we have yet to learn! Their way is already prepared within us; this astral body is much smarter than we are. And so, when it reveals something of itself to us in a dream, it can even appear as someone more clever than we are in physical life. When you consider this— as I will just put in here by way of digression—that will also throw light on the "intelligence" of animals. Animals also have an astral body, and it can bring out what would never normally come into the animal's life. Amazing things can come out in this way. For this astral body contains (whether you believe it or not) all of mathematics, and not only what is now known, but all the mathematics yet to be discovered. If you wanted to read all of mathematics out of it, you would have to actively acquire the corresponding heightened capacities; but it really does contain everything.

When we appear to meet ourselves in a dream, it is the revelation of a piece of our astral body. And much of what we receive as intuitions really consists of such revelations from our astral bodies. Just as, in certain circumstances described above, we may begin to hallucinate, so too, in certain arrangements of our inner organization, something can speak in us that is smarter than we are. Then we can have inner intuitions, and things can emerge in us that wouldn't emerge if we merely applied our ordinary power of judgment in the ordinary physical body. But it is dangerous to allow such things to emerge and to immerse ourselves in them. It is dangerous because we cannot master such things unless we have come by them through the exercise of our judgment. And since we cannot master them, Lucifer has easy access to all these things. We cannot prevent him from directing them according to his own tendencies rather than in the proper direction of the cosmos.

If we strengthen our inner forces, we learn to live inwardly in such a way that we become clairvoyant in the astral body. From what I have said (bringing in the dream as illustration), you can see that such clairvoyance requires a clear concept of this "meeting oneself," or "facing one's own being." Just as in the physical world we are not healthy unless we are fully conscious, in the world higher than the physical world we are not healthy in our soul unless we continually see *ourselves*. In the physical world, you *are* yourself; in the higher spiritual world you have the same relationship to yourself as you do here to a thought that represents a past experience. You can look at this kind of thought; you relate to it as to a memory. And just as in the sense world you relate to a thought, in the spiritual world you know that you are looking at *yourself*, beholding *yourself*. For the things you see in the spiritual world, you must always have *yourself* present as well. And this is, ultimately, the one sole concept that invests all things—and over which, initially, we do not have that power I mentioned earlier; it means that in the spiritual world you master everything; you are the reigning power. Your own being is like the center of gravity around which everything is organized. You can tell, from your own being, how you are in the spiritual world. Let us assume that you are in the spiritual world and you perceive something is amiss; that is, you appear within the occult script as something wrong. You experience your own being and know, "*That* is how you look, since you have done something wrong; now you have to make it right!" You can tell what you have done by how you look. To find an analogy for this, I could say, imagine that you are here in the physical world, but not in yourself—rather, you are all around yourself, and you say to someone, "Now it is 11:30," though that is not true. And in the same moment you would look at yourself, see that your tongue is stuck far out, and think, "That's not you!" And now you start to improve yourself until you can say, "It is twenty minutes after nine." Then your tongue goes back in. So by looking at yourself you can tell if you are behaving well in the spiritual world.

Maybe we have described these things using grotesque imagery, but everyone can sense that they are actually meant in a much more serious way than anything we say about the physical world. This is what it means to use the power of thought we have in the physical world to acquire an initial understanding of supersensible worlds. In this way, we tear thinking free from its attachment to the physical world. In earlier times, human beings had an atavistic, elemental clairvoyance. They could have Imaginations, even Inspirations. But our being able to form concepts about the physical world is a more perfect state in comparison with earlier conditions of humanity. For in the time when humans had an atavistic clairvoyance, they also couldn't think properly. For proper thinking to come about, the power that had once been necessary for clairvoyance now had to be used in thinking. And if today someone develops clairvoyant abilities in some other way than that suggested by spiritual science, then it means he or she has them as an inheritance of earlier times, and has not attained mature judgment for those aspects of life to which the clairvoyance applies. But we are moving more and more into an era for which mature judgment is necessary, and clairvoyance is only to be developed from out of this mature judgment. If someone were to exhibit psychic abilities today, without undertaking serious exercise, and without penetrating spiritual science adequately, then this could mean, not that he or she was evolutionarily advanced, but rather that he or she was backward. You do not have to attain illuminated thinking today in order to develop atavistic capacities in the soul. Which soul is further ahead in evolution: one that only judges in a healthy fashion with ordinary understanding and forms its own idea of spiritual worlds and meanings—or a person who produces all kinds of things clairvoyantly? The more advanced person is the one who has a healthy capacity for judgment. We go furthest astray when we let ourselves be impressed with atavistic clairvoyant capacities. We always make an error when we let ourselves imagine that such a person is a particularly developed soul. A person who exhibits these capacities has not yet undergone certain experiences that have to be undergone while one is still clairvoyant. So the person is catching up with the rest of us. And it is most grotesque when, within the spiritual scientific movement, the presence of these capacities is interpreted as meaning that the person in question must have been a significant personality in earlier times. He or she was certainly a less important personage than someone who has a healthy judgment about things.

Much depends on our having a circle of people who understand all this, and who see through the whole situation. There are "childhood diseases" in all human endeavors, even in the growth of spiritual movements. It is only too easy to understand such "diseases" as they appear within spiritual science, which, after all, provides people with the results of one kind of clairvoyant consciousness. We have had to show that the acquisition of clairvoyance through spiritual science is not so easy and agreeable as the humanity of today and of the future might like. It requires something quite different from simply allowing things to come over you. It requires an every-moment presence, a capacity to take oneself in hand and to observe oneself, as soon as one enters the spiritual world. We need a widespread understanding of how this works. It is far easier and more agreeable to just let something come over you, the way a dream does, surging up and down. We would so much like to relate to the spiritual world in the same way we experience things in the physical world. This tendency is left over from former times, when one actually didn't "know" what one was experiencing in the ancient clairvoyant consciousness; today, too, one might like to experience the spiritual world in such a way as not to "know" it. We underestimate whatever we can know with transparent clarity. For example, when doing sums, we do so by routine methods, without being present ourselves. We add "seven and five is twelve"—without being present for it in the sense meant here, where one has to be present everywhere to make anything so. If you develop a view of the world by yourself, others may not appreciate it. But as soon as you can show people something for which you were not present, they are delighted. If you come and say you know about the spiritual world, since you are present in it, then people say, "Oh, he 'knows' it! But that's a conscious process, so it can't be objective." If you come and say you have observed a phenomenon of light and have no idea how it came about, they say, "That is objective, quite objective! That's believable." But this is the most significant point in our spiritual science, in the spiritual movement that corresponds to true spiritual science, that we try to make clear concepts. Spiritual science is something new, but when the longing for the spiritual world and knowledge of it begins to awaken in human souls, people tend to attach themselves to whatever comes up from the former world of clairvoyance and clairaudience; they think they are doing something special when they preserve these old things. It is our task to see clearly here! We must see clearly the value of completely conscious insight into the spiritual process of healing. But people prefer the dark, delicious feeling that they are receiving communications from the Unknown. Everywhere we hear this kind of cry: "What we can understand doesn't interest us! Bring us something incomprehensible! That is the high thing, the Divine!"

We need not only to draw the individual truths of spiritual science into our souls, but also to have a clear, sure insight into the relationships I have just touched on. I have tried, through a characterization of dreams, to show how real clairvoyance presupposes an intense activation of the soul that can be compared to writing. My book *The Threshold of the Spiritual World* was written to bring clarity into these areas. Whoever understands the book will understand the root, the essence, of our movement. So I must emphasize, once more, that whoever really wants to penetrate into an understanding of the spirit must develop a healthy sense for what is truly scientific and spiritual. Then we will gradually become a society with the task of healing the realm of spiritual life.

We will soon talk further about what we have begun today: a characterization, from out of the spiritual worlds, of the world of dreams.

CHAPTER NINE

Inspiration: Bringing the Unconscious to Consciousness

꧁꧂

FOR STEINER, THERE *are definite stages of spiritual perception. We rise from normal consciousness through Imagination, Inspiration and Intuition. These correspond to heightened, cognitively efficient transformations of thinking, feeling and willing respectively. Here, he suggests that sleep and the afterlife will be perceived differently by those who have risen to the level of Inspiration.*

In particular, through Inspiration we become aware of our pre-earthly existence. It may initially appear from Steiner's references that this means only the existence that happens in the time, the historical time you measure with a calendar, in the years before you were born: that kind of "pre-earthly existence." But here, as in many other of his works (see particularly The Study of Man), Steiner also means something else by "pre-earthly"—a meaning that emerges only gradually. For we re-create our earthly existence every instant. We throw out a world of appearance before us, a world of subject-object distance in which the chair in the corner seems far off, and the other person is a mystery to me. Just "before" this constantly re-created world, however, there is the world of the spirit. The quotation marks are necessary, since "before" refers to a spiritually but not temporally prior existence. Time itself is a feature, not of the spirit that we leave to enter Earth, but of the Earth itself. The "pre-earthly" experience of which we become aware through Inspiration, then, is not necessarily something from years ago, but from light years above.

It is a poetic or spiritual cliche to speak of "light" and "warmth"—quasi-physical characteristics—when describing spiritual experiences. Here, Steiner makes it clear just what he means by these terms. When he says that we are "light within light" in the spiritual world, he means that we exist there as conscious beings, aware of our connection to one another and to the sources of meaning. When he says that we are "warmth within warmth," he means that, as beings of light, we also receive and emit a selfless love.

At the end of this lecture, Steiner will suggest a new and fruitful definition of dreaming: that dreaming is a kind of "blockage." He describes it as something like the ripple that arises when two currents of water meet one another—what physicists call an "interference pattern." During the night, we have been on spiritual adventures; on waking, we return to our body in the bed. The "blockage" or interference pattern that is the dream takes place when the current of our spiritual experience during the night meets the current of thought carried out by our physical and living body.

—————

PENMAENMAWR, AUGUST 21, 1923 GA 227

We pass through our earthly lives in a rhythmic alternation of three states: waking, dreaming and sleeping. Sleep itself is unconscious.

And, though it was of a different kind, human beings in early epochs also had a sort of unconscious sleep state, a state from which no experiences reached awareness.

Yet we are, after all, alive between the time of falling asleep and the time of waking up. We don't die at the moment of sleep; we aren't born afresh on waking. Between falling asleep and waking up we are still alive as soul, as spirit. Yet for ordinary, everyday consciousness, our experience between falling asleep and waking up is completely extinguished. We only recall what we experience while awake, or at most while dreaming, but in normal consciousness we don't remember what we go through in dreamless sleep. The teachers of the ancient mysteries treated their students—and, through the ideas they put forth into the world, the whole of humanity—in such a way that these experiences during sleep became wakeful.

Initiation, as it is now understood, has to remind us of what the human soul experienced before earthly existence. Initiation of ancient times had to remind people of what they experienced every day in sleep. So the teachers of the ancient mysteries arranged their instruction in such a way that their students or listeners could say, "They are only telling us what we experience for ourselves during sleep. We suppress it into our subconscious, but we actually go through it every time we sleep. What the mystery priests tell us is not something unfamiliar; through initiation we have become able to behold directly what normal consciousness experiences during sleep without awareness."

Just as the old initiation wisdom awakened the memory of something passed through in sleep, today it is instead a question of awakening the memory of pre-earthly existence. And this is one of the distinguishing characteristics of ancient and modern initiations. The ancient mystery sages brought nighttime experiences into daytime consciousness, explaining, "In the night, you live with your soul in the spiritual world, which itself lives in every source—in every nightingale, in every flower. By night, you enter into everything that by day you only see from the outside, perceiving it with your senses."

Through this, they could have the conviction that the gods they experienced in a kind of wakeful dreaming during the day were also present in external nature. So by revealing to them the contents of their sleep, the ancient mystery sages demonstrated to their students that divine-spiritual beings are out there in nature. In the same way, modern intitiation has the task of showing people that before they descended to Earth they lived as spiritual beings in the spiritual world among spiritual beings. Through concepts and ideas, through memory, we can recreate here on Earth what we experienced in our pre-earthly life.

In the initiatic wisdom of today, we learn the real distinction between waking and sleeping when we rise from Imagination to Inspiration. What we are ourselves as soul, as spirit, between going to sleep and waking up, only becomes observable to a truly inspired awareness; when we rise to imaginative consciousness, we experience merely the "life tableau." If we develop this life tableau in pure wakefulness, in an empty consciousness, in the cosmic silence as I have elsewhere described it, then our pre-earthly existence can enter our soul as an Inspiration from out of the cosmos. Our own being, our very self, enters our Inspiration at the same time—how this being exists as soul and spirit between falling asleep and waking up.

What remains unconscious during sleep becomes conscious during Inspiration. We learn to behold what we are doing as soul and spirit in the state of sleep, and then we realize that as we fall asleep, the soul and spirit emerge from the physical body and the life body. We leave behind in bed both the physical body and the body of formative forces as I have described it. The higher members of human nature—what we can call the astral body and the actual I-organization, leave these other two "bodies" behind during sleep and re-enter them when we wake up. Only through Inspiration can we really see, really know, this division of our being, which we undergo each time we shift from waking to sleeping. And then we perceive how everything we acquire in normal waking life through our thinking, through the world of our thought, really stays behind in the bed. The thoughts we are at such pains to work out for ourselves during our school years, all our earthly intelligence, has to be left behind with the physical and life bodies when we go to sleep. What we take away with us, as our I and astral body, is quite different from what we experience during the waking state. And what we then experience is something we never normally bring to awareness.

To speak of such things, I have to clothe them in concepts that portray what we normally *experience* but do not *know*. We can ponder them with the "healthy human understanding" of which I have spoken. But this shadowy kind of thinking about things is left behind in sleep, when we enter the world of truly living thoughts, a world in which we do not think the same way we do in the earthly world but rather inwardly experience whatever is there. Unconsciously, we really do experience the light during our sleep. While awake, we think about what the light does, how it allows shadow and color to appear in relation to things; we have thoughts about the light and the effects of the light. But, as we have said, we leave such thoughts behind. In sleep, we pour ourselves out into the weaving, living light itself. During the day, as earthly beings, we carry our physical body, and our spirit and soul, too, through the air and over the surface of the Earth. As sleepers, we enter the weaving waves of light, and we ourselves become beings, become substances, of weaving, living light. We become light within the light.

When you become inspired by what you have experienced every night, that is, when it rises into waking consciousness, then you know that during sleep, you live as a cloud of light within the cosmic light. But this does not mean merely living as a light substance within the light; it also means living within the forces that become *thoughts* in waking life.

The light we experience in sleep is pervaded with creative forces. It is this that works inwardly within plants, within animals, but is also present as an independent spiritual being. You don't experience light as you do here in the physical world. Rather, the living, weaving light is the very body of a spiritual matrix, and also the body of individual spiritual beings. Here in the physical world, we are enclosed within our skin. We see other people enclosed within their skins. There, during sleep, we are light within the light, and other beings are light within the light. But you don't perceive the light as you are accustomed to do here in the physical world; rather, to speak pictorially, the being-like light cloud that we are ourselves perceives another being-like light cloud that is objectively there. And this being-like, objective light cloud is another human being, or some other being that animates the plant world, or a being that has never incarnated in a physical body but exists perpetually in the spiritual world.

So the light is not perceived as earthly light, but as a living spirituality that becomes beings. As you know, we live otherwise here on Earth. We live in warmth; we perceive physically when we are warm and when we are cold, and we heat our rooms when we are cold. So we know that here, for normal consciousness, we live in a sensory way in warmth or in cold. The sensation of warmth or cold is a feeling.

Now, when you leave your physical and life body as you go to sleep, just as you live as light within the light, you also live as a substance of warmth within the substance of warmth. You are not merely a cloud of light, but a cloud of light woven through with warmth, and what you perceive also carries warmth. As a being of soul and spirit in the state of sleep, you do not experience the light as normal light, but as living spirit; you know yourself as living spirituality, and you experience the other beings as living spiritual beings. Something similar holds true for warmth. You cannot manage in the spiritual world, not even for the stage of Inspiration, if you merely bring with you the mental pictures you have attained on Earth. The experience of light within light is actually an experience of spirituality within spirituality; in the same way, when you know yourself as warmth within the cosmic warmth, this is not the warmth you know from the sensory world, but you experience yourself in the world of weaving, surging love. As the being of love that you yourself are in the supersensible, you experience yourself among beings who only draw forth their own essence from out of love. They can do nothing other than have their existence as love within a universal, cosmic existence of love. So you experience yourself between falling asleep and waking up in a spiritually saturated existence of love.

So if we want to enter into these worlds at all, worlds where, after all, we do live every day between going to sleep and waking up, then we must heighten our capacity for love. Otherwise that world remains alien to us. Here in this world spiritualized love does not hold sway; here love is only a drive, drenched with sensuality. In the spiritual world, a spiritualized love is active in the way I have described. And if you want to stand within that world with full awareness, then you have to raise your capacity for love as I indicated yesterday [c.f. lecture of 20 August, 1923, Penmaenwar].

In fact, you cannot find yourself without this capacity for love. For the third of your life passed in sleep would be forever sealed off if you could not investigate it through the development, the heightening of your capacity for love. The form of thinking we develop when we have our physical and life bodies, that is, when we are awake, gets left behind in the bed. While we sleep, our thought activity moves in unison with the whole cosmos. If we could really know what happens in our physical and life bodies during the night, we could also perceive from outside, while living as beings of light and warmth, how the life body continues to think during the night.

We can think even though our soul is far away, since what remains behind in the bed pushes the waves of thought further and further along. It keeps thinking. And when we wake up in the morning, we dip back down into what stayed in bed and kept thinking. We re-encounter our own thoughts in the morning. They didn't just die away between going to sleep and waking up again. We just weren't present to them. Tomorrow, I will show how, when we are not present, we can be far more clever, far more intelligent, than when our soul lives within our thoughts during the day. What gets thought during the night when we aren't there is often much smarter than what we think between waking up and going to sleep again, while our soul is involved.

In any case, I want to suggest today that thought keeps going on in the life and physical bodies and that, when we wake up in the morning and notice a dream, the dream reminds us, in a sense, "When you dive down into your life body and physical body, your soul creates a blockage. There is the physical body; there is the life body, the body of formative forces; and there is the astral body and the I, which dive down into the physical and the life bodies every morning. But when they dive down in this way, something happens like the interference of a thicker wave with a thinner one. It makes a kind of blockage or whirlpool. And this blockage that arises is experienced as the morning's dream. The I and the astral body, which wove during the night in light and warmth, dip down into your thoughts. They do not understand the thoughts immediately but make a mess of them, and this blockage is experienced as the morning dream."

Tomorrow we will consider what else dreaming is, how mysteriously dreaming stands within the whole of human life, and also more about the relationship between sleeping and waking.

CHAPTER TEN

Confronting the Totality of Our Lives through Dreams

FREUD, LIKE MANY others, noted that dreams contradict normal experience. They include all kinds of fantastic events that we never see in waking life. This may seem illogical; it may seem symbolical; current theories suggest that the dream is actually a meaningless sequence of brain events. Steiner, as we may have come to expect, sees it differently.

Here, we read that dreams may indeed be nonsensical if we look at the images and words they contain, but are meaningful if we consider the course, the tendency of the dream. The dramatic flow of the dream resides between the images, between the words—like intervals in music, or weighty silences during conversation. The dream has the almost hopeless task of conveying spiritual perceptions that cannot be fully expressed in earthly terms.

Steiner insists that we do not only seem to leave the realm of natural laws during our dreams, but we actually leave these laws and are governed by a moral universe of beings in communion, rather than a senseless universe of things in opposition.

For the Earth as we know it in waking life is a world of discreet parts, with "everything only connected by 'and' and 'and,'" in the words of poet Elizabeth Bishop. The world of spirit, by contrast, is fluid and immersive, ruled by a communality so light-filled we cannot bear it in normal consciousness. Steiner attempts to portray, by example after example, the kind of unity in which beings and times and events all harmonize in spirit, and how, in the kind of consciousness that is "Earth," they separate out into the world of parts.

———·———

PENMAENMAWR, AUGUST 22, 1923 GA 227

Between waking life and sleeping life (for which I offered at least a sketchy overview yesterday), there lies an intermediary: the life of dreams. This dreamlife, which seems to have so little significance for the immediate reality of every day, has the greatest possible significance for our understanding both of the world and of the human being. It has such special significance not only because spiritual science of the kind practiced here must fully appreciate dreams to move from them to many related topics, but also because the life of dreams presents that opening through which worlds other than our waking world can cast their light. It is precisely the riddle of how dreams are constructed that can alert us not only to the *presence* of other worlds in the depths or heights of the accessible world, but also to *how* these other world might be.

We should realize first that it is extraordinarily difficult to penetrate the riddles of dream life, even from the standpoint of higher consciousness. For dreams can involve a person in the greatest illusions. And we are easily tempted, in regard to dreams, to falsely relate illusion to reality. Let us consider how we do this, taking into account what I have already said about sleep life and about repeated Earth lives.

An example that repeats itself one way or another in dream life is the phenomenon of making something in dream life that you would never think of making in waking life, that you would never be in any position to make in the whole of your previous life on Earth to this point. Then you dream that you have completed this thing and cannot find it; that you search like someone demented for the lost item you think you have made.

Let us consider this example even more concretely. As I have described it, though it may change in each case, everyone has such dreams. Let us say that a tailor dreams, though he is only a poor, lower-class tailor, that he has made a dress coat for a minister. This project makes him feel very happy, and he is soon to complete the coat. But now the dream changes mood, and he is looking everywhere for this coat, since he is supposed to deliver it to the minister, but he cannot find it anywhere.

Here you have a dream that takes place completely in terms that the dreamer cannot carry out in life, but that can certainly be imagined, with wishful thinking, in relation to his earthly life. He cannot carry the project out because in fact he is only a poor tailor for lower-income folk, and you couldn't even order such a coat from him. But maybe in his most daring daydreams, the desire to make such a coat did occur to him. Maybe he couldn't even do it, but the wish is there in his daydreams.

But what is at the core of it? There is a certain reality there. When, with your I and your astral body, you go outside your physical and life body during sleep, then you rediscover yourself as the being who passes through successive earthly lives. What is inwardly powerful and active in your being, while you sleep, is your I and astral body. It needn't only have memories of your current earthly life, but can have memories of other earthly lives. And I am not just telling you something hypothetical, but something that actually comes from reality.

It can very well be that the person in question was involved (say, in ancient Rome in an earlier life) in ordering a particularly stately toga. He need not have been a tailor then; perhaps he was the servant or friend of a Roman statesman. His having had such a lively wish to present his lord to the world in the best way may even have led him to his current profession, since wishes and thoughts have extraordinary significance for the whole of human life. So a memory of something experienced in an earlier earthly life can pervade the soul and spirit of a person—the astral body and the I. Then, in the morning, when the person dives down again, as I have discussed, so that the I and the astral body enter the life body and the physical body, then the soul, which was busy remembering the beauty of the toga, dips down into the images that the tailor can have in his current earthly life—they lie hidden in the life body. Then whatever was experienced of the ancient Roman life gets dammed up, blocked. It tries to enter the mental images that the tailor can have during the day—but during this time he can only have images about making clothes for poor people. It is very hard for the soul, as it descends, to translate what it has felt about the beautiful toga in terms of the dreadful clothes the tailor has to make now. So the image of the toga shifts into an image of a contemporary minister's evening cloak or coat. It is when the person has descended completely into the life body and physical body that his current images erase what he experienced a little while before waking.

So between falling asleep and waking up again we are present to the totality of our lives as human beings. We must confront within us the totality of our human lives with the particular images and thoughts available to us through our experiences in *this* earthly life—and the result is the strange formation we call the dream. This is why it is so hard to distinguish between the content the dreams initially presents, which can be a complete illusion, and the true reality that always lies behind it. This true reality can be something completely different.

You will gradually get used to finding your way in the complex of dream events if you notice that the images conjured up for your soul by the dream are not so important, since these images are formed by the life body left behind in the bed and the thoughts and mental pictures this life body contains. During sleep, though, you actually do not have such images in your inner being. We have to distinguish these contents of the dream from something else, and this I would like to call the dream's "dramatic course." We have to gradually accustom ourselves to turn our attention to the dramatic course of the dream and to ask, "Is the dream moving along in such a way that it would give great joy if the same events happened in real life? Is joy there, is release there, in the dream—or are you sealing yourself into a catastrophe in the dream? Does it move from a certain exposition, where things can reveal themselves, through various complications and then to a fall, a catastrophe?" These are the first questions to ask when considering dream life: not the thought content, but the dramatic flow.

Someone can dream that he is climbing a mountain. The path grows ever more difficult. Finally it comes to a point where the person can't go further, where monstrous obstacles tower over him. He feels that these obstacles interfere significantly in his life. Well, you can have this dream. And it could be painted in more detail. But this person, or someone else, can also have a different dream: He is moving through the entrance of a cave that, for example, leads into a dark mountain vault. Once he has crossed the threshold there is still some light, but it grows darker and darker. Finally he comes to a point where it is not only completely dark, but also the most frightful cold draughts come to meet him so that he cannot penetrate any further into the cave.

You see, here are two dreams with very different content, but they both offer dramatic portrayals of a process that works at the start, then encounters difficulties, then comes to insuperable obstacles. The images are very different, but the dramatic course is the same. For both dreams, the same event in the supersensible world can very well be the source, behind the scenes. Exactly the same thing may have taken place in the soul for both dreams, and it can come to expression in the most varied external images.

All this is meant to show that we need not draw conclusions in an external way, as we do so often, based on the content of the dream. Rather, we need to learn from its dramatic course what the human soul and spirit may have undergone. If, beyond this, we support our conceptual life through the kinds of exercises I have recently described, then we will gradually be able to move from the illusory image world of dreams through the kind of dramatic course I have been describing, to what really lies behind the dream as a supersensible reality between sleep and waking.

Before going into details about the relationship of the dream to the physical body and the human spirit, I want to characterize how, through the world of dreams, we belong to the whole cosmos, the whole universe. We can see, after all, how in dreams we have a completely different connection to the separate events in our lives than the connection we have during waking life. In waking life, as we have just seen in several examples, things relate to one another according to the laws of the physical world. Something later always comes after something earlier, for example. Dreams present what happens in the normal world of the senses, but in a state of dissolution, disorganization. Everything becomes something else; everything loosens and disintegrates. Something bound to the Earth as a being of the sense world, like humans themselves, can suddenly fly. People fly without airplanes in dreams. Something impossible to solve, like a mathematical conundrum, can prove childishly easy in a dream. On waking, you may no longer recall the solution (an unfortunate moment) but you do have the sense that the daytime obstacles to thinking are gone. So everything that has a concrete stability in daily life gets dissolved through the dream. If we want a sensory image of what happens during dreams, or rather what appears to happen, we could put it like this. You take a glass of water and put some salt in it, then you watch it dissolve. Let us even suppose the salt was crystallized, and had specific forms. When we first throw it in, we see the salt in very definite forms. But we then see that the forms dissolve, take on more fantastic, ill-defined shapes, until finally all the salt has dissolved and we again have the appearance of a homogenous liquid.

Something similar happens in our minds, in our soul's experience, with the dream. Both dreams of falling asleep and dreams of waking up remove themselves from daily experience; they dissolve, they body forth all kinds of fantastic shapes and meanings—fantastic from the standpoint of normal consciousness. The dissolution of salt into water is a good image of what actually happens to our soul and spirit during a dream.

For those who have grown deeply embedded in our contemporary way of seeing things, it is extraordinarily difficult to take an unprejudiced view of this fact. For it is especially the self-styled scientific humanity of our time who know astonishingly little about certain things.

None of this is said to cast aspersions on science. That is not my intention at all. I value the scientific spirit and would never want to see dilettantes or non-scientists set in the place of scientific work. From the standpoint of spiritual science, we can acknowledge both the great progress and also the limited truth and certainty of contemporary natural science.

Still, we have to say that today, when people want to know something, they take earthly things and earthly processes. They observe them and draw conclusions from their observations about natural laws. They also make experiments, to learn from them the secrets of nature and to derive natural laws from the results. In this way, you come to a certain kind of lawfulness, and call it science. Then you look out into the expanse of the heavens. You see, for instance, the wondrous spiral nebulae in the heavens, and you see individual heavenly bodies arise and disappear within these nebulae. We can even make photographs of such things today, in such a way as to have much more exact images than we can see through a normal telescope. And what do we do then, to learn about what is happening in the vast reaches of the sky? We take the natural laws of Earth, what we have concluded about the Earth from our experiments, and we speculate how the same laws may have formed such spiral nebulae in the vastness of space. We make hypotheses and theories about how worlds are born and die. And we apply to the heavens what we learned in our laboratories on Earth about earthly magnesium, carbon dioxide and hydrogen. And even when we discover new materials, we make assumptions that lead to highly questionable scientific results. They have found hydrogen and helium in space, for instance, but also another material with a strange name that hints at the confused thinking that goes on. It is called "nebulium." Thinking itself has become cloudy, nebulous, and that is why we have nebulium along with helium and hydrogen. If we just apply what we find in our earthly laboratories in the way of natural laws, and then speculate about what might be going on in outer space after the manner of this Arrhenius,* who has really caused such harm, then we will necessarily fall into one error after another— unless, that is, we take into consideration the following.

Now I want to use another comparison. From natural science, you know how Newton, the English physicist and natural philosopher, established the theory of universal gravitation. He extended

---

* Swedish natural scientist Svante Arrhenius (1854-1927)

the law of gravitation we can see in any falling stone drawn by the Earth, applying it to the relationships between all the heavenly bodies. He also stated that the force of gravitation always decreases with distance.

To satisfy any physicists present, we can state the law as follows: gravity decreases according to the square of the distance, so that at twice the distance it is four times as weak; at three times the distance it is nine times as weak. In other words, gravity decreases according to distance.

It is quite right to set up such a law of force. But you don't have the opportunity, if you stay in physical reality alone, to think about this law in a sufficiently universal way. You think, when you have a heavenly body in view, that its gravitational force diminishes with distance; it is strong, it gets weaker, still weaker, and so on continuously.

It is the same with the propagation of light. Light that radiates out from a light source grows weaker and weaker continuosly.

This is how modern science views the matter. What this view doesn't take into account is that the truth of those natural scientif-

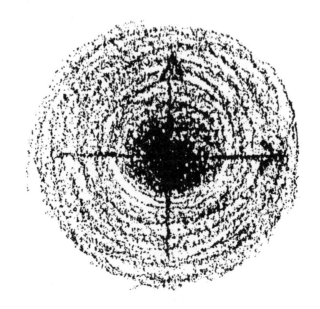

ic laws, derived in laboratories here on Earth, also diminishes the further you travel away from the Earth. So if we establish on Earth a law about the forces binding elements together, or the law of gravitation, the truth of the content of these laws actually diminishes as you travel out into space. And if I have come up with a law here in my laboratory on Earth, and apply it to a spiral nebula in the far reaches of space, then I have done the same thing as if I thought I could light a candle and have its radiance be just as bright out in the spiral nebula as here. I make just the same kind of error when I think that whatever I have found in my laboratory here is also valid out there, in distant space. So it is a far-reaching error for people to transfer the natural laws that may be quite correct on Earth to the distances of heaven.

Yet the human being is included in the kind of lawfulness that comes into play when Earth's laws, like the force of gravitation or the spread of light, no longer apply. To find laws different from our natural laws, in space, you would have to go far out from the Earth. To find them in a more inward, human way, you have to pass from waking into sleeping. When we are awake, we live within the realm of natural laws. Everything we do follows these laws. We decide to lift our hand or arm; the chemical/physical processes in the muscles, the mechanical processes in the skeleton all play themselves out according to the laws we could research in our laboratories or through observation. What lives within the soul leaves the physical and life bodies during sleep. When it leaves, it enters a world that is not subject to these natural laws. This is why dreams make such mockery of natural laws. We enter into a completely different world. We live in this other world, asleep, just as we live in the sense world with our physical bodies when awake. But this other world is very different. It does not have our natural laws, but other laws of its own. Every night, as we leave our physical and life bodies, we dive down into another world where our natural laws no longer apply. And the dream is a force that intensely opposes natural laws.

When I dream, the dream shows me that I am living in a world that protests against natural laws, that doesn't want to succumb to natural laws. When I fall asleep at night and move out of my physical and life bodies, I still live halfway within natural laws; but I am already entering a world that is not ruled by natural laws. So there comes about a confusion of natural and supernatural laws in the dream. The same occurs on waking up.

We can say that each time we fall asleep we dive down into a world where our natural laws do not apply, and with every waking we ascend into the world in which our natural laws do apply. If we really picture this process to ourselves, it looks like this. Imagine that the dream world is like a sea in which you are living. Suppose you wake up out of the waves of dream life in the morning. It is like rising up out of the sea's waves. You move from out of a supernatural lawfulness into the world of sensory/intellectual lawfulness. It is as if everything you see with sharp outlines *after* waking up was born out of something more fluid and fleeting. For example, you see windows here. When you first dream of the window, it too will appear to you as if born out of a flow, from out of something indistinct, perhaps, that has all kinds of fiery flames (see diagram). The window rises up out of these. If you had a very lively dream, you would see how the whole sharp, outlined, definite world of day in your consciousness arises from out of this indistinctness, as if waves rose up out of the sea, and these waves then formed themselves into the daytime world.

And here is one of those points where, if you do research as a contemporary human being, you enter into that awe-filled amazement you can feel in the face of those dreamlike Imaginations of earlier humanity that I described yesterday. If you go back to what earlier humanity experienced in the soul even during waking life in the way of dreamlike Imaginations, to what it formed into the myths and

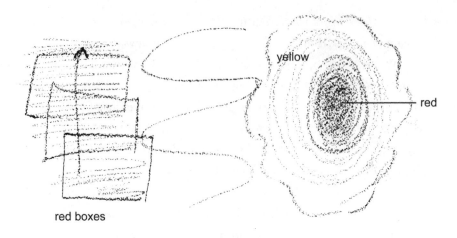

yellow

red

red boxes

legends of the Gods, to what flowed indistinctly in comparison with what we grasp today in our fixed view of nature; if you go back in this way, but equipped with all that we can discover today quite independently of any ancient dreamlike Imagination, then you come to an awe-filled amazement, an awe-filled astonishment, at what lived in the souls of these people of ancient eras. And from out of ancient Greece there still sounds a single word that testifies to the truth of what we can discover here. This word shows that the ancient Greeks still knew something about these matters. It shows that the Greeks said to themselves, "There is something that lies at the basis of the whole universe, and from which all the distinct forms rise forth, but it is something one can only attain if one leaves the sense world and enters the state of sleep, the state of dreaming." The Greek word for this state was *Chaos*. All philosophical speculation, all conceptual investigation into the nature of Chaos is useless. For Chaos is something the human being of today approaches only while dreaming. In the Middle Ages there was still a knowledge of what lies at the basis of all outer substances in the way of a super-natural, hardly material substance. They spoke then of the so-called "quintessence," the fifth element beside the other four—Earth, Water, Air, Fire, and Quintessence.

And something is still present of this when the poet says, "We are such stuff as dreams are made on." The Greek would have said, the world is woven from what you experience as Chaos when you leave the sensory world for a world free of the body. To understand what the Greeks meant by Chaos, we have to point to what lies not in the sensory world, but in the supersensible worlds.

Now we can follow the whole process of going to sleep, dreaming, sleeping and waking up. We can follow it by going into the supersensible worlds along the path described here through Imagination, Inspiration and Intuition. Such a view reveals that the human being shifts, in sleep, from the normal daytime state into a sleep life from which dreams can rise up in an indistinct, chaotic but also wondrous, inwardly unified way. The physical body is left behind in the bed, and with it the life body as the real vivifying, formative, growth-inducing aspect of the physical body. Something twofold is left behind in the bed. Something twofold also leaves the bed and finds its way into that supersensible existence between falling asleep and waking up that I could describe to you today from the viewpoint of the dream experience.

This twofold entity appears to the higher cognition of Imagination, Inspiration and Intuition in the following way. When the person leaves in this way, it is the human being's very own nature, in the form of the astral body. Let us not be dismayed by the words used; we have to have words, and we could take some other term for the astral body. I will shortly have something to say about this astral body, and you will see it is not a question of words but of what ideas we can acquire. The astral body is a sum of processes. Something happens within the human being that goes beyond the physical and life bodies. It is these processes, these events, that are the astral body. In the life body, we left behind the mental pictures, the thoughts. Here in the astral body is spiritualized light and cosmic warmth permeated by the power of love.

What is present in the astral body in this way can enter the life body as we wake up, and form a blockage that appears to us then as the tapestry of the dream. It can also appear this way as it leaves the life body and physical body on falling asleep. It is essentially the astral body that carries us out from the physical and life bodies.

And this astral body is that entity within us that, as I have already pointed out, sets up the actual opposition to the laws of nature. From morning to evening, from waking up until going to sleep again, we are immersed in the network of natural laws that mathematics can describe in regard to space and time. As we go to sleep, we leave the realm not only of natural laws, but also of mathematical laws. We leave mathematics, too, since our astral body does not contain the dead, abstract mathematics of three-dimensional space, but a self-contained mathematics that I could call alive—but spiritually alive. This mathematics proceeds along a single dimension—that of a straight line. I will have more to say about this dimensionality later. But the astral body is actually what frees us from our attachment to natural laws, which we succumb to between waking and going to sleep. Through our astral body, we are transported to a completley different world, the supersensible world.

If we wanted to draw this process schematically, we would have to say: We weave within the realm of natural laws when we are awake (see diagram, white). But the astral body leaves the physical body as we fall asleep (yellow). Here in the physical and life body, our astral body is completely subject to natural laws. In all its movements and processes, it lives within natural laws, as I have shown schematically in these figures (red boxes).

But as it leaves the physical and life bodies, the astral body lives its way into the supersensible world, and now it exists within a different, a supersensible lawfulness. It has become something completely different. Between waking up and going to sleep it wears the straitjacket of natural laws. It goes to sleep—that is, it leaves the physical and life body—and it moves into the world of free lawfulness, which is the appropriate lawfulness for the astral body. It enters a world—that is, it brings us as human beings into a world—that offers free movement to the I, the actual I-organization that is in the astral body and that leaves physical and life bodies with it at the point of going to sleep. The I becomes free in the world the astral body has taken it into. Every night, the I becomes free within a world where it can live and breathe free from the laws of nature.

When at last we stand there between sleep and waking, and our astral body has freed us from natural law, so that the laws of gravity, of the conservation of energy, all these laws no longer apply, then the path is clear for those moral impulses that on Earth, between waking and sleeping, can only exist under the compulsion of world of sense perception. So between sleeping and waking up, the I lives in a world in which moral laws have the same power and force as natural laws have here. And in this other world the I can prepare something; it can prepare what it has to carry out once it has passsed through the gates of death. (We will have something to say about this path from death to rebirth in later lectures.)

Now the I can prepare Imaginations of what it has to accomplish within spiritual reality. Yet these Imaginations are not mental pictures but impulses of power. For when the I has passed through the gates of death, the laws of morality will be like our natural laws here in the physical, sensory world. Here, between falling asleep and waking up, the I, freed by the astral body, prepares in images what has to be undergone between death and a new earthly life. So we can say that the I is already at work, though only in a seed-like way, as if in a tiny spirit-seed, on what it has to accomplish in the spiritual universe after death. And in the images it prepares there lies a hint of what we can take along from this earthly life to the next earthly life—not according to natural laws, but only through the spiritual world. We can only understand the causality of our moral impulses by placing our souls under a certain obedience to them. Because our I works on them in sleep and then again between death and rebirth, these moral impulses attain the same force that natural laws have here, and they clothe themselves within the next human body that we will carry in our next earthly life as our natural moral constitution, as our temperament, as our character, (which is incorrectly ascribed to heredity). So we can see how we are preparing our future, living our way into the future, through our sleep.

And what does the dream show us? I could say, during sleep the I works, but the dream shows us this work in images that are an illusion. What is woven for our next earthly life during the state of sleep cannot be taken into *this* earthly life. The dream, as I explained at the beginning of my remarks today, can show us through confused pictures what we have gone through in earlier earthly lives, as it can also show in chaotic forms what is being prepared, in a seed-like way, for the future of humanity.

So the right interpretation of the dream leads us, in fact, to realize that the dream is something like a window through which we need only look in the right way: a window on the spiritual world. For behind this window lies the weaving activity of the I, which lasts from earlier earthly lives through to future earthly lives. When we interpret the dream rightly, we will be gazing in the right way: from the world of the past, where we live as earthly human beings, through the window of the dream, into the world of duration, of eternity, to which we belong with our own, inner human essence.

CHAPTER ELEVEN

The Logic and Illogic of Dreams

〜〜〜〜

THE PROJECT OF *spirituality is a project of liberation. What seems fixed about the human being proves to be more fluid, more variegated and variable, than we first assume. "The world was fluid and plastic," says Emerson, "in the hands of its creator, and is so still to as many of his qualities as we bring to it." Steiner's lectures on dreams and sleep continually dip into this theme.*

Feelings, like dreams, protest against the rigid sequential logic of normal thought and of the external physical world. Steiner emphasizes that the night, the world of dreams, has something in common with altered states of consciousness generally as they awkwardly approach the spiritual world. Eventually, Steiner will include the inside of the human body, states of automatic writing, feelings and dreams in the discussion. He paints in broad strokes here to emphasize a basic direction and to insist on the multiplicity of the world. He wants us to beware of materialism's bland uniformity called matter. He also takes a swipe, here as in other lectures, against the fig-leaf concept of "the unconscious," a similar blandness that conceals at least as much as it reveals.

———

DORNACH, SEPTEMBER 22, 1923 GA 225

What we learn about the stages of the path into the higher worlds can be mapped against what we already know from normal life. It is a question of seeing the three states of consciousness we normally go through in the proper light. We have often described these three: waking, dreaming and sleeping.

We know how a real waking experience is only present to us in our thinking, in our understanding. We know that feeling operates in such a way that, though it looks different from the world of dreams, its whole relationship to us is similar to that of the dream world. We experience feelings in normal consciousness in just the same indistinct way as dreams, but beyond this we also experience them as having a similar internal structure.

Dreams present image after image. They don't worry, as they follow one image with another, about the connections between things in the external world. They have their own connections. It is the same, at base, in the world of feelings. Someone whose feeling world, in ordinary consciousness, was the same as the world of thoughts would be a terribly sober, dry, icy human being. In the world of concepts—that is, the completely awake world—we have to look to what is, in the normal sense, logical. We really couldn't get far in real life if we felt things the way we think them.

And we have often pointed out that the will emerges from out of the hidden depths of human existence. It can be imagined, but its real essence, how it works and weaves within the human organism, remains as unknown or unconscious to us as the experiences of sleep itself. It would be extraordinarily disorienting for us if we experienced consciously what the will really does.

In reality, the will is a process of burning, of combustion. And to really perceive how our will continually consumes our organism, and has to replace what has been consumed through food or sleep, would not exactly be a comfortable process for normal consciousness to accompany in a fully awake state.

We can to a certain extent put our world of feeling, during waking life, together with our waking dreams and with the dream world of half-sleep, and notice that we experience the images involved as if they were not our "I" but rather something external to us. When we dream, we can feel the dream images as so very much outside us that we even perceive ourselves within these dream images.

But what can interest us most particularly today about these dream images is the following. Normally, we live as if one experience follows the other. In dreams, however, these experiences shift around. The dream disregards the connections between experiences that we have in waking existence. The dream is like a poet with the strangest tastes.

A philosopher recounted that he often dreamed he had written a book that in reality he had not written. In the dream, he thought he had written this book, and it was better than all his other books. But at the same time he dreamed that the manuscript of the book got lost. He rushes through his drawers, looking for the manuscript, and doesn't find it. He has a horrific feeling in the dream that he has lost the manuscript of his very best book and may not be able to find it again. He wakes up in great distress. Of course this was quite an experience for the philosopher I'm thinking of, who had written so many books. So many, in fact, that when I visited him once his wife said to me, "My husband writes so many books that they are in a race with one another."

We all know that a dream does not proceed in the same way as outer life, but that different relationships are forged in a dream. On the other hand, everyone knows that a dream can be intimately connected with what a person really is. In fact, many dreams only mirror the inside of the human body, and we dwell in our dreams as in something intimately connected to us.

Gradually, we become aware of how the dream puts events together in its own way. Looking at the dream as a whole, we can come to realize that we ourselves are present. Now, we live in the state of dreaming either in those moments when we are just leaving the physical and life bodies, or when we again return into them. Dreams actually take place at this transitional point between waking and sleeping, or sleeping and waking. I have often given examples to show that the main thing in dreams is the moment of waking up or going to sleep. I have given as a characteristic example the following (as you will recall): A student dreams that two students are standing at the door of a lecture hall. One says something to the other that (as people say), demands satisfaction, and it comes to a duel. Everything is experienced in a lively way, how they walk out to the duel, the choice of the seconds and so forth, up to the point of shooting. The dreamer hears the shot, but it changes immediately into the crash of a chair that he accidentally knocked over at this moment. So he is waking up at just this moment. The fall of the chair led to the whole dream. The dream took place at the moment of waking up, and it only seems otherwise, since it has its own time within itself—not the time that it would take those events to transpire. Many dreams last longer, according to their own time sense, than the amount of time the person was alseep. Nevertheless, the dream is in intimate connection with the person's inner experience, but especially with what the person experiences in the physical body.

People in ancient times knew of such things very well, and for certain kinds of dreaming—you can read about it in the Bible—the ancient Jews said: God has punished you in the kidneys. They knew that a very specific kind of dreaming was connected with the kidneys. On the other hand, you need only read something like *The Seer of Prevorst* (Justinus Kerner, Stuttgart, 1829) and you will find how people can really describe organic problems out of their dreams. These are people who are particularly equipped for the task; a diseased organ can appear to them symbolically in mighty images, which can even lead to finding a cure. In ancient times this was even made use of, to put the patients themselves in a state where they could name the substance that would heal them out of their own dream interpretation. And what was justified in the ancient "temple sleep" would have to be studied from this standpoint.

If we consider the whole relationship of dreams to outer experiences we have to say that the dream protests against the laws of nature. From the time we wake up to the time we go to sleep, we live in accordance with the laws of nature. The dream, so to speak, thumbs its nose at the laws of nature. And what has been researched as the natural laws of the outer, physical world does not determine the lawfulness inherent in dreams. The dreams contain a lively protest against the laws of nature. If you ask nature what is true, she will answer in natural laws. If you judge the course of dreams according to natural laws, you would have to say the dream tells lies. And dreams do lie in this ordinary sense. And the dream does have to do with the spiritual, supersensible nature of the human being, even if the images of the dream belong to the "unconscious," as we say abstractly. And we judge dreams incorrectly if we do not know they have to do with the inner spiritual reality in us.

Yet this is something that, in our time, is already difficult for people to admit. They want to make the dream abstract. They want to judge it only according to its fantasy images. They don't want to see that in the dream you have before you something connected to your inner life. You see, if the dream is connected in some sense to the inner side of humanity, and the dream protests against the laws of nature, then the inner aspect of human beings itself is something that protests against the laws of nature.

I beg you to appreciate the significance of saying that the inward aspect of the human being protests against natural law. What does this mean?

When natural scientific research observes what is out there in nature through laboratory science, it also approaches the human being and treats humans as if the same natural laws applied to our inward parts—that is, to what happens inside our skin. But this is not the case at all. Dreams, with their denial of natural law, are in a sense much closer to our insides than the natural laws themselves. Our inner life is such that it does not behave and develop its activities in accordance with such laws. And the dream, which is in a sense an image of this human interior, is a witness of this fact. For those who understand, it is simply a fact that has to be admitted. It is ridiculous to imagine that inside our heart, our liver, the same laws hold sway as outside in nature. Logic belongs to external nature. The dream belongs to the human interior, and if you call the dream fantastic, you should also go ahead and call the human interior fantastic. And we can feel how right this is: an illness can crop up in one spot, a sense of well-being somewhere else—truly, between birth and death, our interior proceeds more like a dream than like external logic. But this way of approaching the human interior is completely lacking to our current style of thought, which is completely embedded in what we can observe in our laboratories about external nature. People want to find the same thing in the human interior.

In this regard, it is of great significance that we learn how science treats whatever plays a physical role in the human being. We know that human life requires protein, fats, carbohydrates, salts and so forth. We know all this. Now, what does science do? It analyzes protein, and finds how much carbon dioxide, how much nitrogen, how much oxygen is in it and so on. It analyzes the fates, the carbohydrates, *etc*. But from this kind of analysis no one will ever find out, for instance, what role potatoes have played in European culture. From this kind of chemical analysis you will never discover why rye is digested above all through the forces of the abdomen, while potatoes require for their digestion forces that extend as far as the brain, so that a person who eats too much potato has to use the brain to digest them, and so loses brain forces that could serve in thinking.

It is just in such matters that you realize how neither today's materialistic science nor the more theologically tinted views can approach reality. Science describes food approximately the way you might describe a clock by saying, "The silver came from a silver mine," "The silver is carted to the cities," and so forth ... but stopping at the watchmaker, not looking at what he does. You might talk about the clockface made of porcelain, and where the porcelain comes from. And again you would stop at the watchmaker's shop. This is the way today's science operates when it analyzes food. This is useless, since after all it makes a difference whether you eat a fruit, as in rye or wheat, or whether you eat a tuber, as in potatoes. Tubers enter the human organism very differently from fruits, from seeds. So you can really say that our current thinking no longer penetrates material existence. Materialism is the world view that least understands the ways of matter. Spiritual science has to shed light on our understanding of matter. Those who tend toward materialistic science say that anthroposophy is a spiritual fantasy. And those who have theosophy or theology and stick to the notion of an absent spirit, a spirit that never actually creates, that never shows how spirit has material effects—they say that anthroposophy is materialistic because it dares to understand matter.

So we are attacked on two fronts, by those who want to treat everything abstractly and by those who want to treat everything materially. Those who treat everything abstractly cannot know spirit; those who treat everything as material cannot know matter. So we are descending ever more and more into a style of thought that cannot approach what it is to be human.

Yet in recent times in our spiritual evolution something very remarkable has taken place. Unless people are resolutely stubborn, they have to admit at least the night side of spiritual life. It is characteristic of our time that people embedded in the natural scientific way of seeing things still can't quite deny these darker aspects of spiritual life. A thought-provoking example of this is the book by Ludwig Staudenmaier, *Magic as an Experimental Science*. It is almost as if someone referred to "the nightingale as a machine." Still, that this book could be written in our time is something characteristic, typical.

How does this author actually proceed? The strange thing about him is that his life has led him to approach magic experimentally on himself. He could not deny, after much of what he had experienced, that there are, for example, mediums who channel through writing. You know that I don't recommend such things, and I always talk about what is dangerous in them. But something special happens here, in the case of writing mediumship, where it is important to separate truth from error. For Staudenmaier, this writing of things where you don't know, in the instant of writing, what you are about to write, this channeled writing, became an experimental problem. He started to take up his pencil and behold!, things came out that he had never thought of before. He wrote the most curious kinds of things. Imagine what a surprise it must be when you think in a natural-scientific way, take a pencil in your hand, make yourself into a medium and think that nothing will happen ... but then the pencil takes on a life of its own, leads your hand and writes down all kinds of things that astonish you. This is what happened to Staudenmaier.

What amazed him the most is that the pencil grew moody, as the phrase goes, just as dreams are wayward and moody, and it wrote down things that were very far from anything he had thought. So it appears that at times the pencil directed his hand and had it write things like, "You idiot!"

Now, surely these were things the good man did not think of himself! And after the pencil had written many such oddities, Staudenmaier asked himself the question, "Who is writing all this?"

And the answer was, "Spirits wrote it." For him, this could not be the right answer, since for a scientifically minded man there are no spirits. What should he say now? He can't say the spirits lied to him. So he says his "unconscious" is always lying to him. It is quite a fate, isn't it, to have your unconscious suddenly decide that you are an idiot, and even set it down in black and white?

But he went further, acting as if spirits were talking through him. He asked them why they didn't tell the truth. And they said, "That is our way, we are the kind of spirits who have to lie to you; it's our nature to lie."

This is very typical. And now things start to get tricky. If the truth is above and down below there are only lies, then we have a very uncomfortable situation. But if you are caught in a natural scientific world view, you can only come to the conclusion that the liar is within your own self.

Nonetheless, Staudenmaier comes to the conclusion that it is never objective spiritual entities that are speaking but only "the unconscious." It's the kind of general expression that can cover everything.

But you see, it is actually characteristic of them that these spirits did not lead Staudenmaier's hand to write out a new mathematical proof or to solve a problem in natural science. This is actually what is specially characteristic of them.

Now, Staudenmaier had the opportunity to leave the house for a bit, and he met a doctor friend of his who gave him the advice that he should go hunting. A lot of doctors' suggestions are like this. They like to suggest, for instance, that you should get married. Well, this time the advice was that he should go hunting and get out of this crazy writing business. He should distract himself.

But what happened? Though he now went out and began to hunt magpies and was on the lookout for magpies alone, what looked down at him from the trees were not birds but demonic figures. On one branch there sat something that was half cat and half elephant, and it made faces at him and stuck out its tongue at him. He looked away from the tree to the grass, and he saw not rabbits but all kinds of fantastic figures who played tricks on him.

So it was not only the pencil that wrote strange things, but now his fantasies were stimulated to such a degree that he saw demons and all kinds of ghostly creatures instead of magpies—in other words, more lies. Really what he saw there was like a dream. And if his will had stayed intact he might even have shot at this strange half cat, half elephant creature. If it had fallen, it would certainly have changed again, and become half frog, half nightingale, with a devil's tail. It would have transformed itself as it fell from the tree.

In any case, we can say that this experimenter was approaching a world that is very similar to the world of dreams, and this world is also a protest against the relationships that rely on the laws of nature. What would Staudenmaier's situation have been in terms of natural law? He would have taken his rifle from his shoulder, and after shooting a bird it would have been a bird that fell to the ground. Instead of all this, what happened was, as I have told you, a kind of protest against the laws of nature on the part of this night side of the spiritual world into which Staudenmaier had stumbled. And at the very least, if the man kept to the idea of the unconscious, he would have to tell himself that something down there in the unconscious protests against the laws of nature. What is this unconscious telling him, after all? It is saying something different from what he had thought. At the very least he would have to conclude, "If the world is arranged according to natural laws, then what is within me cannot exist, and as a human being I could not exist. For when my interior speaks, it goes completely against natural laws." We belong, in our inner life, to a completely different world than the world involved in the "laws of nature." It is a world that protests against these laws.

This is really the only interesting thing about this magical experimenter or this experimental magician, who has impressed so many people.

CHAPTER TWELVE

Dreams and Human Development

〜〜〜〜

IN THIS LECTURE (*reproduced in part*), *Steiner introduces the life of dream in an important context. Sleep and dream are not held up here as ends in themselves, nor as reliable indicators either of what is going on in the world or of what is going on in the supersensible aspects of the sleeper. Instead, sleep and dream are represented as sites in which to search for clues to the spiritual background of life on Earth: where we have been, where we are now and where we are going.*

Steiner inveighs here against our normal use of language. It is a theme that permeates his lifetime of writing, lecturing and leading spiritual discussions. For language has gone through a certain evolution, and brought us through our own evolution as separate selves, but our task now is to find the thinking beyond words that can truly reunite us to one another, to the Earth and to divinity. In Anthroposophical Leading Thoughts, still being written in the last days of his life, Steiner points to a heavenly realm independent of earthly languages that is both the source and the future of human understanding.

Dreams, like language, are to be understood not in their products but in their processes. Just as we must ignore the individual words in order to grasp the meaning of the sentence as a whole, so we must ignore the individual images in a dream in order to grasp the "dramatic course" of the dream—which is a purely spiritual quality that could clothe itself in innumerable dream images. Steiner hints at the dream stream, the vast flowing source, normally inaccessible to awareness, that gives rise to the dreams we normally remember.

What we bring with us from other realms on entering this life is akin to what we bring down with us from the heavens each morning in the way of dreams. Since the fifteenth century and the birth of the modern physicalist mindset, we have tended to neglect, or rather not even to notice, the feel-able, will-able sacred images that accompany us at birth, or every morning on waking into what John the Evangelist calls "this world." Steiner wants us to grow curious about the sources of our minds, and even the sources of our nighttime mental wanderings. In doing so, he points us toward the spiritual worlds outside what currently passes for psychology: the world of the heavens, above normal consciousness, and the world of evil, which lies below it.

DORNACH, SEPTEMBER 11, 1920 GA 199

. . . Today, we live in a period of human evolution in which we ourselves must become inwardly active to contribute what we can to a necessary shift in the nature of the will. For it is our own human soul substance that will have to overflow and turn outward, into objective outer life. We are the ones who have to make things happen. We can no longer wait passively by, as if divine beings far away from us, without our aid, could affect human evolution.

We can understand such things in the details of both social and natural life, though today our focus is on social life. I would like to start with something quite specific. Let us suppose that someone announces himself somewhere, sends his business card, for example, and on the card you read, "Edward Miller." Now, who would assume that this Edward Miller is actually a miller, who grinds grain into flour? Maybe he's an architect, or a professor, or a senator, or what have you. No one is justified in assuming anything based on the name Miller; more likely you wouldn't think anything of it, but wait until you found out something about this Miller. Or you might know from some other circumstances who it is who bears the name of Miller.

In a case like this you can see how wrong it would be to conclude, from the name Miller, anything about the person who bears the name. If someone is named Smith, we don't assume he's a smith in a smithy. So with proper names we know we have to do something to find out what's behind the name.

But proper names have gone through a certain development to get to this point. Someone named "Smith" today has nothing to do with a smith. "Miller" has nothing to do with being a miller. But the names do come, originally, from the time when, in the villages, before family names existed in the same way as today, people said, for instance, "Smith said it"—and they really meant the smith. Or they said, "Miller did this" or "said that" or "I just saw Miller." Anyone who has lived in a village knows that family names are often neglected, and instead people say something like, "Miller's here." So, once upon a time, you called someone by a name that let others know what was behind the words.

The path these proper names have traveled—a trajectory we can supervise in complete clarity today—is the same course that all our words, our whole language, will travel in our current transition from the fifth to the sixth post-Atlantean civilization. Nevertheless, today we still take nearly all our wisdom, all our knowledge, out of language. At base, with regard to the majority of our language, we still deduce what is being talked about from the words themselves. It may seem easy to judge the content from the words, but the course of human evolution points in a different direction, and we have to relate to such things as we relate to the phenomena of nature. There are objective necessities involved in such matters, even in regard to that region of life that many of us experience in airy abstractions and respond to accordingly. For it often comes to the point I have mentioned before: "Yes, I didn't want this or that; I didn't mean it; I meant it differently; I had this or that intention." But no matter how much we don't want to be burned, if we reach into the fire we get burned anyway. It is not our intentions that decide things in life, since intentions aren't deeply enough *in* life. What matter are only those intentions that are deep within life, or else just facts and the lawful relationships among facts.

Based on spiritual scientific understanding, it is absolutely necessary to accustom ourselves to this way of thinking. So we have to accustom ourselves to the idea that, even if it would be easy to stay with words, the objective course, the objective lawfulness of human evolution says otherwise. Our whole human constitution, our whole inner life, is freeing itself from words. More and more, words are becoming just pointers that hint at what is being said, but they don't explain it completely. If you are serious about your spiritual science, you will have to face a fact that has made many people angry at me: You will not be able to use words and sentences in the normal way for our time. In representing spiritual science you are representing something from the future, something that has to become a general human possession in the future. You have to accept, into your will, something that will appear in the future. So you have to speak of things in such a way that your words point and hint at what is really behind them. And since what we think of now as the formation of our society must be born from spiritual science, we have to speak in the same style about social development. This is why people did not want to understand my book *Towards Social Renewal*. They wanted to find something there in the old style, but it couldn't be written in the old style because it's about the future. And what we're talking about here can be seen in the fact that the questions about *Towards Social Renewal* that came from many sides always proceeded from the old style of thinking, and no one even tried to find a way to the new, transformed thinking.

So in the representation of all the social relationships of the future, we have to dive into this emancipation of our soul life, so that it no longer clings to words. Whoever has followed my recent spiritual scientific writings and lectures will notice that I always try to explain things from the most varied sides, and that as a rule I use two sentences instead of one because one sentence hints at one side of the issue and the other at the other side. So listeners or readers then have the feeling that they should approach the issue beyond the words, beyond the sentences. This is what has to be said about the change in our relationship to language and its relationship to our inner life. And it is important, because the majority of the confusion that comes into our thoughts and concepts today actually derives from nothing other than this: the objective, lawful impulses of human evolution already demand that we liberate ourselves from language, but people are attached to their familiar habits of thought and don't want to let go of language.

Clearly seen, this kind of phenomenon leads to a deeper under-standing of the whole course of humanity. From this transformation of our language, or our languages, we can build a bridge to highly spiritual matters. Of course, it is more the case for one language than for another. But it is then a question of the individual treatment of language, of linguistic meanings, in the specific, differentiated areas of human civilization.

Now we are within the fifth post-Atlantean period, and we are approaching the sixth. We cannot draw sharp boundaries between these periods of development, but the peculiarities of the one reach into the other, and the following age, before it arises, throws its shadow—or its light—far into the preceding epoch. You have to grasp these lights if you want your soul to participate in human evolution. Now we want to bring this super-historical fact of our working towards the sixth post-Atlantean civilization into connection with the other fact, also known to us all: that we descend with our soul-spiritual nature out of a spiritual world into earthly incarnation through birth or conception, that we then live our lives on Earth between birth and death, that we then pass through the gate of death, and that in passing through the gate of death we take our spirit and soul back into the life that consists entirely of soul and spirit.

We have to be clear about something that is also very significant for the art of education, namely that we bring down with us, from out of the spiritual world, whatever we have experienced in this spiritual world. Just as when we go from one place to another we take with us not only our clothes but our soul and spirit, so too through birth or conception we bring with us, out of the world of soul and spirit, the results, the effects of what we have gone through in the spiritual world. And in the period that humanity has just now lived through, the period that began in the middle of the fifteenth century, human beings brought their soul and spirit with them but devoid of images—they brought forces of soul that had no images. This is why intellectual life arose in this time period; intellectual life blossomed. Something was imprinted on people before physical birth, or before conception, that had no qualities, no images. This is also the reason for the lack of original fantasy in the creative activity of the time since the middle of the fifteenth century. For fantasy is, in fact, only an earthly reflection of super-earthly Imagination. The Renaissance is not a counter-argument here, precisely since it was a re-naissance and not a "naissance," not a birth. Original fantasy was not present; rather, there was a kind of fantasy that needed to be enriched out of earlier times. In short, the soul became permeated with imageless forces. And now there begins something that accounts for much of the storminess of our times. There begins a time in which the souls out of the spiritual world are bringing images with them as they descend to Earth at birth or conception. Images, if they are brought along out of the spiritual life into this physical life, and if they are to promote the well-being of human social life, must definitely connect with the astral body, while everything imageless connects with the I. And it has been above all the I that has blossomed in human affairs since the middle of the fifteenth century. Now the time has begun when we have to feel that images live within us from before our birth, and we have to make them alive within us during our lives here. You can't do it with just your I; it has to work its way deeper into you. It has to work its way into your astral body.

For the most part, we resist the entry of these images we experienced before conception into our astral body. We push away to some degree everything that rises from the depths of our beings to enter into our astral body. The sobriety, the prosaic quality of the current age is a fundamental characteristic, and today there are even broad movements that oppose our concern, in education, for allowing what is in the soul to rise up into the astral body and make itself felt. There are dry, sober types who really want to exclude from education the myths, fairy tales and everything permeated by fantasy. In our Waldorf school system it is a priority for teaching and upbringing to proceed from imagistic portrayals, from the living presentation of images, from legends and from fairy tales. And even what children learn at first about nature and the processes that take place in the animal kingdom, in the plant kingdom and in the mineral kingdom, are not said in a dry, sober style but are clothed in images, in legends, in fairy tales. For there sit deep within the children's souls those Imaginations they have received in the spiritual world. These images want to rise up. And the teacher or adult who relates to the child in the right way will provide images to the child. And when the teacher places images before the child's soul, such images arise—or more exactly, the *force* of images that were actually received before birth.

If this is suppressed, the dry, sober teacher of today will bring in just what our young children don't feel any relationship to: letters. For letters, as we have them today, have nothing more to do with the old image-letters. They are something absolutely foreign to the child, and they are something that really should be drawn out of an image, as we try to do in Waldorf schools today. People are bringing imagelessness toward the child today. But children have in their bodies (I mean of course in their—the astral body, as we say), they have in their bodies certain forces that will burst the body if they are not drawn out in imagistic portrayals. And what is the result? These forces don't just disappear. They spread themselves out, they make themselves felt, they crop up in thoughts, in feelings and in impulses of will. What is the result for us? Rebels, revolutionaries, discontents, people who don't know what they want because they want something that cannot be known; they want something that is incompatible with any social structure, something that they only imagine, that should have become part of their fantasy life but which instead becomes part of their social misconduct.

Those who, in an occult sense, are not quite honest with their fellow human beings simply don't trust themselves to say: If the world is going through revolution today, it is actually heaven that revolts. It is the heaven that is held back within human souls, and that comes out not in its proper form but in its opposite; it emerges in battle and blood rather than in Imaginations. It is no wonder that the people who participate in this kind of social destruction have the feeling that they are doing something good. What do they feel within themselves? They feel the heavens within themselves—only heaven takes on a caricatured form in their souls. The truth we need to examine today is serious. To acknowledge these truths is not some kind of child's play. It has to be approached with the very greatest seriousness. It is not easy to speak of such things, first because people don't like to hear them, and second because people are attached to words. If someone says that heaven is going through a revolution in the human soul, he or she is interpreted according to the words, and no one notices that the speaker first tried to show that you have to know something else—that here the word "heaven" is connected to something other than its accustomed meaning, just as when Mr. Miller is announced and you have to understand that it doesn't mean he grinds grain. This liberation from language is certainly necessary in actual cases if we want to move forward according to the demands of human evolution.

So we see how something from our life before birth finds its way into our social life. And if you know how things are connected to each other, you know that what appears here on Earth in caricature is a version of something heavenly. This was about the social realm. But there is still a further step to take.

In the time of intellectualism, which has developed above all since the middle of the fifteenth century, people also received extraordinarily little in the way of Imaginations out of their sleep life. Even those who had somewhat livelier dreams tended to explain these dreams quite rationalistically, quite intellectually. Theosophists, for example, are rationalistic and intellectual in this area. How many people have come to me over the years and wanted rationalistic explanations for their dreams! It would take a thick book to describe them all.

The issue here is that even the Imaginations that live in our dreams point to a still deeper life of the spirit. I have often said that dreams do not depend on externals. They have already liberated themselves from their actual content. And what we receive in the way of dream contents, and then transfer into the words of a language (from which we should really free ourselves), is not the true course of the dream at all. It has frightfully little to do with the true course of the dream. The content of the dream is the dramatic course of the dream, how one image follows upon another, how points of tension are knotted and then released, so that the same spiritual content can be experienced in many ways. One person comes and says he climbed a mountain and could climb very well up to a certain point, then suddenly he stands in front of an abyss and can go no further. Another reports that she was walking along, happy with everything around her. Suddenly, at a certain point on the path, someone approached her with a knife and killed her. Two very different dream images! But the spiritual process behind them may be the same. It comes out one time as the climbing of a mountain and the feeling of standing in front of an abyss, and the next time as the process of walking along happily until you meet someone who wants to kill you. It is not so much a question of the content of the images, but rather of their dramatic course, of how you encounter and go through something in the dream. It is a matter of the inner dynamic that lives behind these images; that's what matters. The same play of forces can clothe itself in these images, in other images, in hundreds of images.

We only begin to understand the spiritual world when we realize that what plays itself out here in the physical world as dreams, or whatever comes from the spiritual world in the form of images similar to the physical world, that all of this is, in fact, only an image. But as long as you have the inclination to interpret images rationalistically, in a purely reasonable way, then you will approach even your dream life in an intellectualistic way. What matters is that we begin to understand the dreams in our sleep life as the expression of a deeper spiritual life. Only then will we approach it Imaginatively; only then will we realize the images are themselves the content. And then we will not be in opposition to what is beginning for humanity: that is, the process of putting inner, soul challenges to ourselves from out of sleep in the same way as Imagination does before birth or before conception.

The fact is, we are beginning to sleep differently today from the normal sleep of the intellectual period since the middle of the fifteenth century. During all this time, we have had very little inclination, when we awaken, to simply experience the images and not interpret them. Now we are at the point in human evolution where we can take Imaginations from out of our sleep as well. These Imaginations do not want to live into our I alone, where reason rules, but also into our astral body. If we work against this, then we are pushing away something that wants to emerge into awareness from out of the depths of the human soul. We are working against the whole course of human development. And it matters that we not work against human evolution, but with it. We work in the proper direction when we fill our current culture as much as we can with whatever is connected to the spiritual world. Of course, in terms of outer life, what matters here is that we permeate ourselves with whatever we understand from out of the spiritual world. We permeate ourselves with real spiritual cognition, with whatever is in the physical world but cannot be understood in terms of the physical world. The whole recent period of human existence strove against this. Let us consider a particular case I have often mentioned before.

Christianity, after all, came toward humanity in such a way that it can only be understood, that is, the Mystery of Golgotha can only be understood, if humanity embraces an understanding of the supersensible. For we have to imagine that a being who previously was not united with earthly evolution, such as the Christ, united himself with the human being Jesus of Nazareth, so that supersensible processes took place. We have to imagine that even birth and conception were different in the case of this Golgotha event than for normal human lives. In short, there are challenges presented by

Christology that require us to understand it in a supersensible way. There is an interesting point where one of our newer natural scientists is inveighing against the immaculate conception and says that to claim there could be an immaculate conception is to arrogantly dismiss human reason.

Well, that is how the modern rationalist, the purely intellectualistic person, has to see things. In a certain sense, what comes from the spiritual life is indeed an arrogant dismissal of human reason. What matters now is that we are living in an age where we have to manage to bring what is experienced spiritually between falling asleep and waking up into our waking life. We must do so in such a way that our astral body—not our I, which is the seat of reason, of intellectualism—becomes permeated with images. And it is interesting that even the theology of the nineteenth century has developed in such a way that it set Christology in opposition to rationalism, to pure intellectualism. More and more, modern theology felt entitled to deny Christ as such and to set up the simple man of Nazareth, Jesus, as a merely human personality who was somewhat above the average. They didn't want to bother understanding something supersensible. They wanted to understand what is trying to approach us supersensibly, and is supposed to awaken us to the supersensible, in terms of concepts that can be attained here in the sensory world.

. . . We are beginning in our time to bring something different with us through conception and birth than we have been doing since the middle of the fifteenth century. We are beginning to bring something different with us out of sleep when we wake up each morning. Both of these developments challenge us to look at things attentively, so that we really penetrate to an understanding of such a decisive event as the Mystery of Golgotha. How could you ever attain an understanding of such an event without spiritual science? External education, external science, never even approach the issues involved. They just pass them by; and according to their methods, they have to pass them by. It is a bitter thing to see the discrepancy between the inner challenges posed by our human evolution and what we bring toward these challenges from our side. The recent challenge has been for us to take account of what is flowing into us from out of the spiritual world. Instead, we came up with the idea of atoms, molecules and so on. We came up with the idea that every body extended in space reduces to atoms. But out of the very sources of our human evolution the necessity has arisen for us to encounter the realm of spirit. . . .

CHAPTER THIRTEEN

Interpreting Dream Images

FROM THE TIME of his fundamental philosophical work, *Intuitive Thinking as a Spiritual Path*, Steiner pointed to elusive but knowable aspects of human existence. Sleep and dreams are just such aspects. It might seem that we already know them adequately, that we have observed them adequately, and that we are then free to reason and "understand" them on the basis of such observation. But Steiner challenges us with the results of a more intimate observation.

Strangely, but also wonderfully, Steiner never says in detail how he comes to his observations. Over and over, he points to the path of meditation in general, the path as outlined in his books, *How to Know Higher Worlds* and *Outline of Occult Science* and in the philosophical works themselves. What he does not give, however, is a "path of dreams," a dream yoga, with specific steps by which to make the same observations that he has done. Rather, he begins this lecture, like many others, with relatively familiar aspects of dream or sleep and then moves quickly on to other areas more difficult for most of us to follow. How shall we approach such things?

Thus, when he makes an analogy between a person's forcefulness in life and the quality of his or her dreaming, we can more or less follow him. *The force of character required to mold a life seems to rhyme with the plastic quality of lively dreaming. But when Steiner writes that our dreams are seeds for a future existence, or when he points to the link between experiences during Imagination and the formation of the body's physical organs before birth, then we may wonder about its relevance to us.*

On the one hand, such "information" about the spiritual world and its workings is not really information at all, but an invitation to enter the realm Steiner indicates (see Kühlewind's Working with Anthroposophy*). In that sense, the descriptions of other worlds and bizarre processes are not relevant to ordinary consciousness, but might be quite relevant to meditative consciousness.*

On the other hand, it is fruitful to let fall away many aspects of the lecture as you read it, while keeping for contemplation only those thoughts, those phrases even, that do in fact "speak" to you. It is like panning for gold. You take in the gold and ignore the sand. What is sand for you, or the you of today, may prove golden to someone else, or to the you of another day. No matter. Your attention is rightly held by what inspires you now, what just now draws you to your edge, and even beyond your edge.

DORNACH, FEBRUARY 8, 1924 GA 234

I have already alerted you to the contrast between the states of waking and sleep. You know of it in ordinary consciousness, and through it you can really find a way—one of the ways—to approach the deep mysteries of human existence. For out of sleep there wells up *life*, the life of the soul, the life of the dream. It is a kind of life that normal consciousness quite rightly does not take too seriously, as long as one has no hankering for the mystical, or anything like that. There is a certain justice in it when sober folk refuse to take dream life seriously, since they see how it shows all manner of images and memories out of normal life. And if they then compare their experiences in normal life with the life of dreams, they naturally keep to normal life, and declare it their reality. The dream world comes along with its variations on the normal experiences of reality, and in our normal consciousness we cannot answer the question: What meaning do our dreams have for the total life of the human being?

Let's examine this dream life as it appears to us. We can distinguish two quite specific types of dream. One kind conjures up images of external experiences before our soul. Either recently or long ago, we may have experienced this or that, and we experienced it in a particular way. The dream conjures an image out of sleep that is either like or unlike these outer experiences—generally unlike them. If, nonetheless, we realize that this kind of dream image is connected to an external event, then we see how very different the outer event becomes in the dream. For the most part, though, we experience a dream image and never relate it to this or that experience in the outer world, because we don't notice any similarity. But if we approach our dream life more closely (this kind of dream life, which conjures up altered images of outer experiences before the soul), then we find that there is something within us that takes hold of the experiences. Still, it cannot grasp them in the same way as when in waking consciousness we make full use of the organs of the body and images arise in the memory that are as similar as possible to external life. In memory we have faithful images of outer life, or at least more or less faithful images. There are also people who "dream" in their memories, but this is an abnormality. In memories we have more or less faithful images of life. In dream images we have altered images of outer life. This is one kind of dream.

Another way to dream is actually much more characteristic for an understanding of the life of dreams. For example, someone dreams of a row of white columns, one of which is broken or dirty. The man wakes up out of this dream and notices he has a toothache. And he realizes that the row of columns symbolizes a row of teeth. The one aching tooth is the broken or dirty column. Or the person wakes up with a dream of a hot oven, and notices his heart is beating fast. Or a person is anxious in the dream because a frog is approaching her hand; her hand then grasps the frog, which is soft. The woman shivers in the dream. She wakes up and has a corner of the bedclothes in her hand; she had taken hold of it while sleeping. But it can go much further. The person dreams of snake forms; she wakes up with intestinal pain.

So we realize that there is another kind of dream, dreams that express the inner organs of the human being in a pictorial, symbolic way. Once we learn to recognize how certain dreams, with their strange images, are symbols of inner organs, then we can learn to interpret much of the dream images in this sense.

In a dream, you enter a vaulted cellar. It is dark overhead, with spider webs everywhere. It is a horrifying sight. You wake up and realize you have a headache. The headache, the inside of the skull, became the vault of the cellar. You can even notice that the folds of the brain are expressed in the peculiar architectural forms that make up the archway of the vault. If we pursue our investigations in this direction, we find that every organ can appear to us in dreams in this imagistic way.

And there is something in this that points very strongly, through the dream, to the whole inner life of the human being. There are people who, while dreaming, invent the themes of wonderful paintings, for example. Anyone who studies this area knows what inner organ is captured, changed and symbolized by such paintings. There is an extraordinary beauty in such paintings at times. And when a painter then hears which organ is really being symbolized by such beautiful paintings, he or she may be quite shocked—since the organ is not as respectable as the painting!

These two kinds of dreams can very well be distinguished from one another if you only allow yourself to investigate the dream world intimately. In one form of dream, we have to do with images of external experiences we have gone through as human beings in the world. In the other kind of dreaming, we have to do with imagistic mental pictures of what is within us.

Now, up to this point it has been relatively easy to put forward our observation of the dream world. And most people who are alerted to these two kinds of dreams will be able to recall that their own experiences justify this categorization of dreams. But what does this distinction of two kinds of dreams really point to? If you look at the first kind of dream and notice the particular images it uses, you realize that the most various outer experiences can be represented by one and the same dream, and that one and the same experience can be represented in various people by various dreams.

Suppose someone has a dream in which she comes to a mountain. There is an opening in the mountain, a cave. The Sun shines into it up to a point. The dreamer goes in, feeling her way further. She comes to an obstacle. She feels there is a little pond in her way. She is in grave danger. The dream takes a dramatic course.

Such a dream can represent the most various external experiences. It can relate, for example, to the fact that someone was in a train accident. Years later it may be symbolized in dream experiences whose images are completely different from the experience in the train. The same dream could represent a disaster at sea, or a friend's unfaithfulness, and so on. If you compare the dream image with the expereince, and proceed with an intimate observation, you find that the content of the dream images actually has no great significance. But the drama, the flow, is of great importance: whether there is anticipation, whether the anticipation leads to resolution, whether the anticipation leads to crisis. All the relationships of feeling become transposed into the life of the dream.

And if, going forward from this point, you study a person in regard to the first kind of dream, then you find that these dream images get their character from the whole way a person is, from the individuality of the person's I. If you understand dreams—not "interpret dreams," but actually understand them—then you can often get to know someone better through them than if you only observed their outward life. Still, if we look at everything the human being encompasses with this type of dream, it alerts us to what the human I experiences of the outer world.

On the other hand, if we consider the second kind of dream, we can say that what gets conjured up before the soul in these dream images is experienced only in the dream. While awake, we experience at most the outward form of our organs through the sciences of anatomy and physiology. But this is no real experience at all; it is an external view, of the same kind we direct to plants and stones. We need not concern ourselves with it further. So by the kind of consciousness we go through life with, we experience amazingly little, or nothing, of our inner organism. But the dream of the second kind conjures up for us (in altered images to be sure) our whole organism.

If we then observe a person in life, we find that this life is controlled by the I, more so or less so according to the person's strength of will and character. And we find that the way this I takes effect in a human life has an extraordinary similarity to the first kind of dream experience. Try to test this for yourself. If someone has dreams that strongly, vehemently change the corresponding outer experiences, you will find in him, or in her, a person of strong will. If the dreams show life almost as it is, with no distortion, you will find a person of weak will.

So you see, by the way in which you form your dreams you express the way your I takes effect in your life. We have to bring the first kind of dream into relationship with the human I. And when we consider how the I and the astral body are outside the physical and the life bodies during sleep, then it should not surprise us to learn from spiritual science that it is the I, *outside* of the physical and life bodies, that takes hold of the images of life in a dream—images that the I takes hold of in outer reality *through* the physical and life bodies. The first kind of dream is an activity of the I outside the physical and life bodies.

What is the second kind of dream? Of course it also has to do with what is outside the physical and life bodies during sleep. It cannot be the I, since the I knows nothing of the dream's symbols of the organs. We are forced to recognize that it is the human astral body that forms these symbolic images of the inner organs, just as it is the I that forms the images of outer experiences. And so, in these two kinds of dreams, we have an indication of what the I and astral body are doing during our sleep.

We can go further. If we see what a weaker person does in a dream and what a stronger person does, how a weaker person dreams things almost as they happened, while a stronger person changes things, throws them into a muddle, and makes them bear the stamp of his or her own character, then we can compare our findings with the way the person behaves in waking life. And then you come to something incredibly interesting. Let someone tell you his or her dreams, and notice how one dream image joins to the next, how these dreams are formed. And then, after you have a mental picture of how this person dreams, and have imagined what you could of his or her dreams, you will have a good image of how the person is in life. You come upon some remarkable human mysteries. You observe people as they behave in life; you get to know them as individuals. You say, "What happens through these people expresses only a part of their actual human nature or I. If the whole I were involved, they would do what they dream. Powerful people, if it really were a question of their I's, would change their lives as much as they change their dreams. Those who allow their lives to continue almost unchanged in their dreams would pull back in dreams, too, let life alone, let things be, and interfere with life as little as possible—only as much as they do in their dreams."

And what is the source of what happens in human beings above and beyond all this? My dear friends, it is easy to say: God does all that; the spirits of the cosmos do all that. For we human beings actually do not do everything by ourselves; we do only as much as we dream. The rest is done through us and to us. Only normally we don't learn about such things in life. If we did, we would see that we have only as active a role in life as we do in our dreams. The world prevents powerful people from being as powerful as in their dreams. In weak people, it is the instincts that are active, and again it is life that adds what happens through them—what they wouldn't dream for themselves.

It is interesting to look at how people behave in life and to ask yourself: What really comes from them and what comes from the world? What comes from them is exactly as much as they can dream about a given matter. The world either adds something to it, in the case of the weak, or subtracts something from it, in the case of the strong. Looked at in this way, the dream starts to be something extraordinarily interesting, something that lets us look deep within the nature of a human being.

Some of what I have been saying has occurred to the psychoanalysts, though in a distorted, caricatured way. They cannot see into the actual warp and weft of human nature, and so they distort everything and turn it into a caricature.

But you can see from the view that I was able to put forward today, even if quite externally, that to understand these things at all you would have to achieve a very sensitive understanding of the soul. Without this, you cannot know anything about the relationships between the dream life and the external reality that a person lives. That is why I once said that psychoanalysis is dilettantism, because it knows nothing about external human life. But it is also dilettantism because it knows nothing about internal human life. And these two dilettantisms don't merely add up, they mulitiply, because not knowing inner life spoils the outer life, and not knowing outer life spoils everything inward. If you multiply d by d, you get dilettantism squared. So psychoanalysis squared is $d \times d = d^2$.

If you enter intimately into the alternating states of waking and sleeping life, you can see so deeply into human nature that it really leads to the science of initiation.

Let us take something else I have said recently: that through practices of the soul, through meditations, we can strengthen the forces of our soul and move forward beyond our normal, more or less contentless abstract thinking to an inwardly visible, imagistic thinking, to Imagination. As I have said, with Imagination you progress to the point of viewing your whole life, as it was established in the Earth as a life impulse through birth and conception—actually before birth, before conception. Through your dreams, you receive resonances of what you have experienced outwardly since entering this earthly life. Through Imagination, you receive images that feel very similar to dreams images, only they contain resonances of what came before earthly life.

It is silly for those who do not know spiritual science to say that your Imaginations could also be dreams. They should think over what gets "dreamt" in Imaginations. For their content is nothing from the senses; they portray the nature of the human being before the person had any senses. Through Imagination, we are led into a new world.

But there is a distinct similarity between the second kind of dream and what is experienced in Imagination, as this Imagination is first formed through exercises of the soul. For you experience images with great power, clarity and exactness; you experience a whole universe of wondrous images, colorful images, images so powerful that consciousness contains nothing else. If you wanted to paint them, you would have to paint a vast tableau; but the painting would only show an instant—in the same way it is impossible to paint lightning, but you can fix an instant on canvas, since everything goes by in time. But if you were to hold fast a moment in this way, you would have a glorious image.

Let us proceed schematically. Naturally, it is not a question of any great similarity with what is beheld supersensibly. But to bring the matter before our souls we want to represent it schematically (see diagram).

Consider this picture, which I have drawn here schematically. It has an inner structure. It contains the most varied contours. Inwardly and outwardly, it is something vast. If your concentration grows stronger and stronger, you will be able to hold this image for longer, and it will not just arise for an instant. To do so, you have to grasp it with real presence of mind as it emerges for an instant, otherwise it disappears before you have made it present to yourself at all. To observe the spiritual at all, you need presence of mind. So if you develop presence of mind to the point not merely of having it in consciousness at all, but to the point of keeping it steady, then the image draws together until, instead of something that spans the universe, it becomes smaller and smaller and you see how it moves forward in time. I could even say that it collapses into something; from out of one part it becomes the human head; another part becomes the human lungs; another becomes the human liver. The physical matter from the mother's body only fills out what actually stems from the spiritual world. And so the human being emerges. Finally

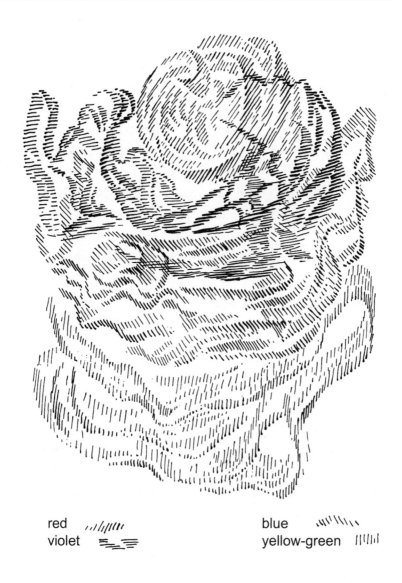

red ⫽⫽⫽⫽⫽   blue ⫽⫽⫽⫽⫽
violet ═══   yellow-green |||⫽|

you can say to yourself, "Yes, we see in a vast image in the pre-earth-ly existence what the liver really is; we see the lungs in pre-earthly existence in this great image." And now you can compare it, in ret-rospect, with dreams of the second type. There an organ appears to you, as I have said, perhaps also as a very beautiful image; but it is still a stunted thing in comparison with what Imagination offers.

And so we have the impression that the Imagination offers something created out of cosmic genius; the dream offers something stunted. Yet both point in the same direction. They both represent the inner organization of the human being in a spiritual form.

From here it is not a big step to another, very valid idea. When through Imagination you perceive this pre-earthly human being as a vast life image, when you see how it becomes crystallized down into the physical human being, then you tend to ask the following question. What if the dream images that relate to inner organs were active in the same way as the organs themselves? Then you would have, for instance, the caricature of your liver. The human liver, perfect in itself, is formed by the Imaginative image relating to pre-earthly existence. If the dream image became your liver, you would not receive a human liver from it, not even a goose liver, but the caricature of a liver.

This gives us insight into our whole essence as human beings. For you see, it is clear that there is something very similar between the Imaginative image and the dream image. And you can ask: Where does the similarity come from?

But we can go still further. Take the first kind of dream image, which relates to outer experiences. In this case, there is no initial similarity with the Imagination. The concepts of Imagination refer to our pre-earthly experience, where we had nothing to do with other physical human beings; Imagination refers to the impressions of pre-earthly spiritual experiences. Consider what this means.

When we look within the human being, we get the impression that certain symbolic images, whether they arise through Imagination or through a dream, indicate the interior of the human being, of the human organism. On the other hand, Imaginations that relate to outer experiences are connected neither to the inner organism nor even to outer earthly experiences; they indicate the experiences of a pre-earthly existence. We can compare these latter to the dream experiences that relate to outer earthly experience, but have no inner connection to them. This inner connection is present for dreams of the second kind.

Now, what is the point of all this? By portraying all these things I wanted to show that there is a intimate way of examining human life, which really presents us with important riddles. It is a fact that we look at life today in a very superficial way. If we looked at it more closely, more intimately, we would notice the things I have spoken of today. But in a certain sense these things do occur to us, only we know nothing of them consciously. We really never realize what a powerful influence our dreams have on our lives. We think of dreams as something that breezes past us because we don't know that our I is active in one form of dream, our astral body in the other. But if we try to comprehend our lives in regard to even more significant phenomena, then the riddles of our existence become still thornier.

Those who have been with us for a long time have already heard about these facts. I want to indicate again that there is a pathological human condition in which a person cannot retain a coherent memory. I mentioned how I once knew a man who, without any awareness of what he was doing, left his home and his family, went to the train station, bought a ticket and traveled to another station like a sleepwalker. He got a transfer at the next station and went further, then repeated the process. He started his trip in southern Germany; they later found out he had traveled to Budapest, to Poland, to Lemberg, and so on. He finally came to himself—his awareness started to work again—in an asylum for the homeless in Berlin, his final stop. But up to this point of awakening there were several weeks in which his awareness was extinguished. He remembered the last thing he had done at home; everything else was gone. They had to find out where he had been by external methods.

You see, in such a case the person's I is not present to what he or she is doing. If you look into the literature, you will find that there are hundreds and hundreds of such cases where the consciousness of the I is missing. What is really happening here? If you could study the dreamlife of such a person, you would find something remarkable. First of all, you would find that, at least occasionally, he or she had the liveliest dreams, dreams characterized particularly by his or her having undertaken something, having had some intentions, in the dream.

If you study the dreams of a healthy person, you will find that this involvement with intentions is either very weak or altogether absent. A person will dream about all kinds of wonders, but normally intentions play no role. When intentions play a role in dreams, the person usually wakes up from such dreams and finds them very silly.

But if you study the dreams of people with intermittent awareness like this, awareness that gets extinguished for periods of time, then you will see that they set up intentions, goals, aims in their dreams and then take these intentions very seriously when they wake up. They take them so seriously, in fact, that they experience remorse if they can't carry out the intentions they formed in their dreams. Sometimes these intentions are so foolish, in relation to the outer physical world, that they cannot carry them out. Then it bothers them and troubles them. This is the other side of the extinguished consciousness: taking the dream seriously, in particular with regard to the dream of intention—not the dream that expresses a wish, but the dream that expresses an intention.

Someone who knows how to observe people can sometimes tell if someone might go through a period of extinguished awareness. Such people have something that shows they are never altogether awake with regard to certain inner and outer experiences. You can gradually come to see that every night, while asleep, such people leave their physical and life bodies with their I and go too far out, so that they cannot bring back everything they have experienced out there. They go too deeply into the spirit to carry back all they have experienced into their physical and life bodies. And, finally, because they cannot bring it all back, it keeps them "out." What they have experienced too deeply in the spirit finally holds their I back, out of the physical body, and they enter a state where the I isn't in the physical body at all.

In this kind of radical case where a distubance of consciousness appears, it is particularly interesting to observe such a person's dream life. It is different from the dream life of most of our contemporaries—and much more interesting. Only, of course, this interest has its other side. But just as illness is more interesting than health, when observed outwardly (not when seen from within by the person in question, if they have an understanding of the human essence)—so too the dream life of the kind of pathological person I have portrayed is much more interesting than the dream life of—I won't say of Philistines—of our contemporaries.

So we do find a kind of link between the I and the whole world of dreams. I would almost like to say you can grasp it, this connection of the I with the dream world. And the following questions arise: How is it with the dream images that relate to inner organs, in relationship to the Imaginations that relate to these organs? How does all this work?

First of all, what is given in Imaginations in the way of images of our inner organism points to what the human being contains before having an earthly body, before coming to Earth. Dream images only arise once the person is here. So Imaginations point backward; dream images point to the present. Now, it is true that a normal dream image, which relates to an inner organ, is a caricature of the inner organ, while the Imagination of it corresponds to the inner organ in its perfection. Still, we can say that this caricature nonetheless has the possibility, within itself, of growing into the organ itself.

We can tell ourselves, as we consider the caricature, that it could grow into a perfect organ.

Now, this is the beginning of a course of thought that we will continue tomorrow, and that is rooted in the question: Does that which the Imaginations offer point to a human being's past life? And is the dream the beginning of the Imagination of the future? Could it be that from today's dream images there rise the Imaginations that we will look back to in a future earthly life? Is the content of the dream in some way the seed of the content of the Imagination?

We are face to face with this significant question. And so we see what we have been able to attain in our investigation of dreams draw near to the question of repeated earthly lives. As you can see, too, we have to look into human life more deeply than is normally quite comfortable if we are to find a link with what the science of initiation has to say about the essence of the human being.

Through a lecture such as today's I wanted to show how superficially we look at things in our current civilization, and how we need to develop an *intimacy of observation*. But this kind of intimacy leads to spiritual science.

CHAPTER FOURTEEN

Dreams: The Human Essence in Spiritual Connection

IN ORDINARY CONSCIOUSNESS, *we fail to experience the meaning of our dreams. In fact, we fail to experience dreams themselves, for we have to do always and only with the memory of a dream. We wake up and the dream is already over.*

But dreaming is a different matter, according to Steiner, for those who have achieved a higher stage of consciousness. They feel the dramatic course of the dream behind its manifest content, and so begin to "lift the veil" of the dream, to sense a spiritual meaning, a living presence, behind and within it. In a sense, it is one's own essence one sees in the dream. This applies, we must remember, not to normal awareness, but to those who have reached what Steiner calls a more "light-ful" kind of awareness, inwardly ordered and convincing. And, very surprisingly, Steiner suggests that to such an awareness the dream can reveal something of what human beings will become in the future.

He uses an analogy here that is most helpful: the analogy of the seed to the mature plant. Just as the old plant withers around the forming seed, so our body is, in a sense, an element of decay, coming as it does in its form from out of our earlier lives, while the dream can be seen as the seed of a new life.

Steiner goes further, and in a characteristically exact and poetic passage contrasts the head, the rhythmic system and the limb/metabolic system in terms of their liveliness and of the kind of cognition necessary to understand them. It would require tremendous cleverness, out of Imaginative consciousness, he says, to begin to understand the head, while to grasp the limb system we need to sleep or dream, and to understand the rhythmic system we must swing between waking and sleeping.

Steiner goes on to consider the tableau consciousness that develops through a vastly heightened power of memory, so that all our lives are with us in a single great picture. This leads to a consideration of the hidden side of these experiences of ours, their meaning side. Life is something like a book whose letters we see but whose language we have yet to make out. Through spiritual scientific practice, we begin to feel the debt we owe the gods through our non-understanding of life. It is a debt, Steiner emphasizes, that we can make good only after death.

For during waking life we know only the human side of our deeds on Earth; in deep sleep we unconsciously experience these same deeds from a God's-eye point of view. After death, we run through our experience again in reverse, spending about as much time on this review as we spent sleeping during our life on Earth (that is, about a third of earthly life). For it is the sleep experiences we most need to review, containing as they do the spiritual perspective of all we have known on Earth. "Only what we lived through each night unconsciously, we now live through consciously."

DORNACH, FEBRUARY 9, 1924 GA 234

Yesterday I tried to show how, through a more intimate observation of the life of dreams, we can draw close to the science of initiation. It will now be my task to deepen what I portrayed yesterday from the standpoint of normal consciousness. Today I will look at the same subjects as yesterday, but from out of Imaginative cognition, that is, as things can be seen when viewed by someone who has managed to view the world in Imaginations.

Let us initially disregard the difference between the two kinds of dreams I described yesterday. We will take dreams as such. We arrive at a valid view if we picture how Imaginative life, Imaginative sight, behaves in the face of a dream dreamt by someone gifted with Imagination. And we can compare this with the self-observation of such a person with regard to his or her own human nature—whether the person is seeing his or her own organs Imaginatively, or those of another person, or the whole person as an organism.

You see, both the dream world and the physical and life bodies seem very different to Imaginative consciousness and to ordinary consciousness. The Imaginer can also dream, and these dreams may sometimes be as chaotic as those of other people. From out of his or her own experiences, though, such a person can very well evaluate the world of dreams, since alongside the imaginative life, which is an inwardly ordered, inwardly light-ful life, there flows the world of dreams just as it does alongside ordinary consciousness.

As I have often emphasized, the person who really achieves spiritual sight is not a dreamer or sentimentalist, living only in higher realms and never seeing outer reality. Someone like this, always dreaming in higher worlds, or of higher worlds, is no initiate, but is probably mentally ill. Real initiatic knowledge does not lead away from normal physical life and its particular relationships, but on the contrary makes us more careful, more conscientious observers than we would be without the capacity of second sight. And we can even say that someone who has no taste for normal realities, no interest in the details of life, no interest in the details of other people's lives—someone who hovers in this "exalted" way over normal life and doesn't worry about details—all this is sufficient proof that the person in question has no clairvoyance.

So the person of Imagination (I include here of course Inspiration and Intuition as well), knows very well about the life of dreams from his or her own experience. But there is a difference in how dreams are experienced. The person who can Imagine feels the dream as something with which he or she unites, with which he or she becomes *one* much more than this can take place in normal consciousness. The dream can be taken much more seriously. And it is really only Imagination that can justifiably take a dream seriously, since it is capable of looking behind the dream, to some extent, and to sense the dream's dramatic course, its tensions and relaxations, its catastrophes and crises, rather than to focus too much on the particular dream content. After Imagination, the content of dreams becomes less interesting. It is much more interesting whether the drama leads to a crisis, whether it leads to joy, whether it leads to something easy or something difficult, and so on.

I have to repeat that it is this sequence, this drama of the dream, that begins to be most interesting—just the part that often seems uninteresting to normal consciousness. If you can begin to see behind the curtain of the dream, you notice that the dream presents you with something that connects you to your spiritual essence in a very special way. You can say that a dream is actually the human essence in its spiritual connection, as we can say of a seed that it *is* the plant. You learn to see, in the course of the dream, the seed of a spiritual human essence. And you learn to know, in this seedlike human, something that is alien to the current life. It is alien in the same sense as a plant's seed, taken from it in the autumn, is alien to the plant's grown form. The seed only comes into its own in the next year's growth. And this consideration of the dream offers the most powerful impressions to Imaginative consciousness, since in one's own dreaming nature one comes to sense, more and more, how one carries within oneself something that passes over into the next earthly life, something that grows forth between death and rebirth and continues growing into the next earthly life. You learn to sense, in the dream, the seed of your next life.

This is extraordinarily important. It is confirmed when you compare this powerful experience, a feeling experience, with the view you can have of the physical human being standing before you equipped with all the individual organs. Imaginative cognition perceives this person differently, so that you get a feeling similiar to what you have when a plant you knew as a green, fresh, blooming plant begins to wither. With Imaginative consciousness, as you consider this lung, this liver, this stomach, this brain as physical organs, you have to say to yourself that, compared with the spirit, all this is in a state of decay.

You will object that it is must be unpleasant to consider the physical human being, through Imagination, as something beginning to wither. But no one who has come to know the science of initiation will claim that its purpose is to present us just with what we might find pleasant. It is supposed to give us the truth. But on the other hand we have to point out that by knowing the physical human being as a decaying being, you are seeing the spiritual human being. You cannot, in a sense, see the spiritual human light up if you don't learn to know the phyiscal as a decaying, withered being.

This does not make a person appear uglier, but rather more beautiful and also truer. And if you can observe the spiritual decay of the human organs, then these organs with their life content appear as something that has come over from the past, from a previous earthly life, and that is now decaying in the present life. In this way, you

really come to the idea that within the decaying human being—
decaying from out of the previous earthly life—the seed is forming
for the future life on Earth. What decays most is the human head.
And the dream appears to Imaginative consciousness precisely as an
outflow from the human head.

What decays least, by way of contrast, and is almost like the normal dream in this way, is the metabolic and limb system. It is least
decayed, and most connected as to form and content with the person's future. The rhythmic system, all that is hidden in the cavity of
the chest, makes the link between the other two. It holds the balance.

To spiritual vision, the heart in particular becomes a remarkable
organ, seeming to wither, but staying almost (though not quite) the
same. Only to a spiritual-Imaginative view it appears more beautiful,
more noble, than in its form as a physical heart.

And so there is a certain truth in it when, to paint an image of
the spiritual view of the human being, a relatively wise, even elder-
ly face is linked with childish feet and hands and even wings to hint
at distance from the Earth. And yet the heart is also indicated in
some fashion, and it resembles the physical heart.

If you have the Imaginative view of the human being, then
painting something in this way is not "symbolic" in the negative,
empty sense in which we use symbols today. Rather, it contains elements of physical being that at the same time raise themselves apart
from physical existence. And we could say—for we have to start to
speak a bit in paradoxes if we speak about the spiritual world, since
the spiritual world looks completely different from the physical and
so appears paradoxical—we could say, once we begin to regard a person with Imaginative cognition, that we have the feeling, with
regard to the head, "Oh, how cleverly I would have to think in order
to be a match for this human head!" If you study the human head
through Imagination, you gradually begin to seem very weak-mind-
ed to yourself. For the very sharpest thoughts developed in normal

life cannot easily master this wondrous formation of the human head as a physical construction.

By contrast, if you want to understand the limb and metabolic system with Imaginative consciousness, then you can say to yourself, "My sharp reason is no help here at all; I have to sleep and dream about a human being." In regard to these organs, a person is best understood by being dreamt about—in waking dreams.

So you see, you have to move into a very differentiated kind of looking to investigate the human being Imaginatively as far as the physical organism goes. You have to become clever, frightfully clever, to investigate the head. You have to become a dreamer to investigate the metabolic and limb system. To understand the marvelous formation of the rhythmic system you have to swing back and forth between waking and sleeping. But all of it is revealed as the vestige of an earlier earthly life.

Whatever we experience of ourselves while awake is the vestige of an earlier earthly life. It only plays into the current life in the way I said yesterday, for example with regard to one's actions: we really complete by ourselves only as much of our actions as we can dream; the gods do everything else. To this extent, then, the present plays a role; everything else comes from previous earthly lives. You can see this in someone when you perceive the physical body as decaying. And if you can behold what people know about themselves while they dream (in sleep), then you see what they are preparing for their next earthly life. You can make such distinctions very clearly.

By considering the human being in sleep and awake, Imagination leads us to a view of the development that passes from one earthly life to the next.

Both in sleep and in waking, the element of our souls known as "memory," remembering, has a very special place. Consider your normal memories. You know that what you remember you draw forth from yourself as thoughts, as mental pictures. You form mental pictures of past experiences. You know that in such memories the experiences lose their liveliness, their colors and so on. Experiences pale in memory. But on the other hand, these memories have to be acknowledged as very strongly connected to the essence of the human being, or even as *being* this essence. Only we are not normally honest enough to admit what we have to admit in this direction.

But I ask you: If you look within to find out what your I really is, then what is it if not memories? Looking for your I, you will scarcely find anything else within you other than memories of your life. To be sure, you will find that the memories are permeated by a kind of activity, but this remains very shadowy and dark. It is memories that appear, in a lively way, to be our I.

This world of memories, which you need only ponder for a moment to have before you in its whole shadowy, soulful quality—what does it appear to be for Imaginative awareness? It opens out before the Imagination and becomes a vast tableau in which you have a pictorial overview of everything you have experienced in this earthly life. We could say that if this is the human being [Steiner draws something on the board], and this is the memory, then through Imagination memory spreads out all the way to the time of birth. You feel yourself from outside, from space, and everything in space is a happening, an event. You gaze into a tableau with an overview of your whole previous life. Time becomes space. You look into it as you would look down a long avenue, a panorama, and you can say that memory has spread out, extended itself. In normal consciousness, it seems to be only a moment. For example, if you are forty years old and you recall something from twenty years before, you don't normally Imagine it, but rather form a mental picture of it. It is as if you were far ahead of it, in space, but it is still present. And when you Imagine, you know that it has stayed there; it has not disappeared—any more than a faraway tree in a line of trees. So you gaze into this tableau, and you realize that this memory carried in normal consciousness is a mere illusion. What normal consciousness bears in the way of memory is a kind of reality—in the same way that the cross section of a tree can be taken for the reality of the tree trunk. This one cross section is really nothing: it is only a very partial image, while the tree trunk itself extends both above and below it. And you find something like this when you grasp memory through Imagination. You realize the whole emptiness of separate contents of memory; the whole of it is spread out before you as far as birth, and sometimes beyond birth. Everything past becomes present. It is present; it may be as distant as the periphery, but it is there.

And once you have grasped this, once you have this kind of view, then you learn something you can continue to investigate indefinitely: namely, that a short time after death, when you leave the physical body, this tableau becomes your very life. When you pass through the gates of death, for several days you have this experience of looking into the panorama of your life; you gaze upon it in luminous, shining, powerful images.

Now it is necessary to proceed further with Imaginative cognition. You can then enrich your life in a certain way; you see things in a new way. For example, let's say you consider how you behave toward other people. You consider the intentions you have in mind for your actions, for how you behave toward others. Now, in normal life you may think over a particular event to some extent, depending on whether you are more or less thoughtless, but you always have a mental picture of your own behavior. However, it is really only a partial image. Now, in this new way of seeing, it is all present to you.

Let us suppose that you did something good or bad to someone else. In normal consciousness, you will see success from a good deed, the contentment of the other person; perhaps the other person will have been furthered by your help. In other words, you will see the kind of results of your behavior that can appear in the physical world. If you have carried out an evil deed, you will be able to see how you have harmed a person, how that person grows dissatisfied, how you even injured a person physically and so forth. All of this can be observed within the physical world. But this is still only one side of the matter. Every action we take toward another human being, and even the actions we take toward the other kingdoms of nature, has another side to it.

Let us suppose, for example, that you do someone a kindness. This good deed has an existence within the worlds of spirit; it has a certain meaning. It is a source of warmth in the spiritual worlds; it is like the point of origin of spiritual rays of warmth. In the spiritual world, warmth of soul streams outward from a good deed performed for someone else. Coldness of soul streams forth from an evil deed done to another person. And so it really is as if you bring spiritual warmth and spiritual chill into the spiritual world according to how you behave toward other people. Certain other kinds of human behavior act like rays of brilliant light in the spiritual world, while still others give off darkness in the spirit. In short, we could say that on Earth we only experience half of what we are doing.

If you enter into Imaginative consciousness, then everything known by the other, normal consciousness disappears. Whether you have harmed or helped someone is the affair of normal conscious-ness. The effect of an action on the spiritual world—whether it is warmth or coldness of soul, light or darkness of soul—rises up before Imaginative consciousness. And you can say to yourself, "The only reason this wasn't present to me before is that I let my normal con-sciousness operate during my actions." Only please don't imagine that because you weren't aware of them—of these sources of radiant warmth and light of soul—they were not there. You experienced them, but unconsciously. You went through it all. Just as your eyes, that is, the eyes of your soul in higher consciousness, see it now, so too while you were carrying out a good deed for the benefit of anoth-er, while you were carrying out an evil deed that harmed someone, your unconscious moved on a parallel and knew exactly what the deed meant in the spiritual world.

And the moment you advance far enough in Imaginative consciousness for it to be sufficiently intense, you not only see the panorama of your experiences but are also obliged to notice something else. You see that you are an incomplete human being if you don't experience this other side of your actions, this other side of your earthly life. You begin to seem crippled to yourself, in regard to this life panorama that reaches to birth or beyond, as if something had been hacked off of you. You continually say to yourself, "You should have experienced this side of things too; you are like someone missing eyes or missing a leg; you are not a complete human being. You haven't really had half of your experiences." This has to come about in the course of Imaginative consciousness. You feel stunted in regard to your own experiences; you feel that ordinary life has been hiding something.

In today's materialist civilization, this is particularly common, since materialism doesn't believe that human actions have any further value and meaning than what they seem to have immediately in external, physical life. People consider it nonsense if anyone asserts that something else is going on in the spiritual world; yet this is in fact the case. And for Imaginative consciousness, this feeling of being crippled does arise. You say to yourself, "You really have to give yourself the opportunity to experience what you have not experienced." But then we almost never do it—or only rarely and inadequately.

This is the serious burden borne by those who see more deeply into life. They see that, finally, they have much that they have not been able to fulfill in this life, and that they are in debt, in a sense, to the future. We have not been able to experience all that life has obliged us to experience. We owe the completion of these tasks to the universe, and we realize that to experience all that we should, we will first have to go through the gates of death. This is a powerful, yet often tragic enrichment of life given by the wisdom of initiation. We see our unavoidable debt to life, and the necessity of writing an IOU to the gods, telling them, "I can only experience this once I have died; only then can I enter into the kind of experience I owe to the universe."

This awareness that the inner life has to occur in part in the form of an exchange against the future, after death, deepens human life immeasurably. Spiritual science is not only here to learn this or that theoretically. If you study spiritual science in the same way as you study other things, you would be better off reading a cookbook. Then at least you would be compelled not to read it theoretically. Life itself—and particularly the life of the stomach—ensures that you will not read a cookbook theoretically. Spiritual science too has to deepen life in terms of our feelings, our hearts.

There is an immeasurable deeping of life in noticing this debt we owe the gods and in saying to ourselves, "We actually cannot experience half of our lives on Earth because it lies hidden under the surface of life." If, through initiation, you come to know what is hidden to normal consciousness, then you can see a bit of *what* you owe. And you realize that with ordinary consciousness you may be aware that you are in debt, but you cannot read what's written on your own IOU. With initiatic consciousness, you can read the IOU, but you cannot pay it in everyday life. You have to wait for death. And if you have achieved this consciousness, if you have deepened your human conscience to the point where this awareness of debt is very lively, then you are ripe to pursue human life after the retrospective tableau of which I have spoken that goes back to birth. And you see how it has to begin after a few days: that you have to experience what you left un-experienced.

For every single deed you did to another person or to the world, you now have to experience what you left out before. The very last deed you did just before death comes up first, then you go back through life. You become aware of the cosmic significance of the good or evil deeds you did. What you experienced of them on *Earth* is now missing; what you experience now is what they mean for the *universe*.

And it goes further. You experience your life in reverse. You know that during this period of experiencing life backwards, experiencing the universal significance of this life, you are still bound to the Earth because it is only the other side of earthly deeds that you experience.

You then feel as if your further, future life were borne within the womb of the universe. What you experience is a kind of embryonic stage for the further life between death and rebirth, only that you are not borne as an embryo by a mother, but by the universe—that is, by the universe of what you did not experience here in physical existence. You live your life again in reverse, but in terms of its universal significance. You do so with a sharply divided consciousness. When we live here in the physical world and look at the creatures around us, we feel like kings. Even though we say the lion is the king of beasts, as humans we feel still higher. We feel the nature of the other kingdoms as somehow beneath us. We can judge these other kingdoms, but we don't imagine that they judge us. We feel differently once we have passed through the experience I have described as coming after death. We no longer feel exalted above the other kingdoms of nature. We feel that there are other spiritual kingdoms, and that we are beneath them. We feel like the lowest, while these others stand above us.

And as we pass through what we have previously not experienced in this way, we feel all about us the beings who are exalted above us, and whom we are beneath. These beings bring their sympathies and antipathies toward what we experience of our earthly lives. In this experience after death, it is as if we are in the midst of rain, a spiritual rain. We experience our deeds once again in their spiritual aspects, but now the sympathies and antipathies of exalted beings rain down around us. We are drenched, permeated with these sympathies and antipathies. And as a spiritual essence yourself you have the conviction that whatever the sympathies of these exalted beings of the higher hierarchies shine on will be accepted into the universe and eventually add good to the universe; whatever their antipathies fall on will be rejected.

An evil deed done to other human beings is soaked by the antipathies of these beings. And you feel that this linkage with their antipathies would mean something extraordinarily bad for the universe if you did not in some way bind this evil deed to yourself—if you released it from yourself. And so you gather up whatever is met by the antipathies of these beings.

This then forms the foundation for Karma, for what operates into your next earthly life, so that it can find compensation through other deeds.

It is possible to portray this passage of the human spirit through the soul region more from an external standpoint, as I have done in my book *Theosophy*. There it is all put more according to our current way of thinking. Now, as I recapitulate, within the General Anthroposophical Society, what anthroposophy is as a system, I want to portray matters more inwardly so that you can sense how a person experiences the after-death state as a human, as a human individuality.

Now, having seen all this, we can cast a glance back at the world of dreams and see it in a new light. Once we can see how, after death, we experience the spiritual side of our earthly existence, of our earthly deeds, of our earthly thoughts even, then we can look back at our experiences of dreaming and of sleep in a new way. We can realize that during sleep we already experienced all this, but unconsciously. And we see the difference between the experience of sleep and the experience we now have after death.

Consider human life on Earth. There is the waking state, and it is continually interrupted by sleep. If you aren't too much of a sleepyhead, you will pass about a third of your life asleep. And during this third of your life you will pass through this other, spiritual side of your existence, but without knowing anything about it. The dream only tosses up tiny wavelets. You notice a something of this other side in dreams, but it is only a superficial wavelet. In deep sleep, on the other hand, we experience completely unconsciously this spiritual side of daily life.

We could even say that in conscious daily life we experience what people think and feel, how they are helped or hindered by us. In sleep, we experience unconsciously what the gods think of our deeds and of our thoughts during waking life; but we know nothing of it as it happens. This is why, once we can gaze into life's mysteries, we seem to ourselves so stunted, as I have described, and so burdened by guilt. Everything stayed so unconscious for us! After death, we really run through it again, only consciously. And this is why that part of life we slept through is experienced once again—that is, about a third of the time of our earthly life. After passing through death, we experience our lives again night by night; only what we lived through each night unconsciously we now live through consciously. We could almost say, though it might seem we are joking about these extraordinarily serious matters, that if you sleep through most of your life, then this after-death period lasts longer; if you only sleep a little, the time is shorter; on the average, it lasts a third of your life because you slept a third of your life. So if you live sixty years on Earth, this experience after death lasts twenty years. And during this experience you go through a kind of embryonic life for the spiritual world.

And once you have gone through it, then you are really free of the Earth. Then the Earth no longer surrounds you like a sheath. Then you are really born into the spiritual world that you will live in between death and rebirth. So you feel it as a birth in the spirit and you slip free from the husks of earthly existence. . . .